An Introduction to Literary Semiotics

Advances in Semiotics Series
General Editor, Thomas A. Sebeok

# An Introduction to Literary Semiotics

by

MARIA CORTI

*translated by Margherita Bogat and Allen Mandelbaum*

Indiana University Press/Bloomington and London

Translated from Maria Corti, *Principi della comunicazione letteraria* (© 1976)
Published by arrangement with Bompiani, Milan
Manufactured in the United States of America

Library of Congress Cataloging in Publication Data
Corti, Maria.
An introduction to literary semiotics.
(Advances in semiotics series)
Translation of Principi della communicazione
letteraria.
Bibliography: p. 161
Includes index.
1. Literature.   2. Communication.   I. Title.
II. Series: Advances in semiotics.
PN45.C6513      801'.9      77-23650
ISBN 0-253-33118-8   1 2 3 4 5 82 81 80 79 78

# Contents

Parmi ces hommes sans grand appétit de Poésie, qui n'en connaissent pas le besoin et qui ne l'eussent pas inventée, le malheur veut que figurent bon nombre de ceux dont la charge ou la destinée est d'en juger, d'en discourir, d'en exciter et cultiver le goût; et, en somme, de dispenser ce qu'ils n'ont pas. Ils y mettent souvent toute leur intelligence et tout leur zèle: de quoi les conséquences sont à craindre.

Valéry, Oeuvres, I, 1283

# Foreword

In every study, the vantage point from which the object of that study is considered is the operative choice of the critic. That choice makes certain forms of inquiry more pertinent than others, which would be valid from another perspective. This statement, however, is less self-evident than it seems, because no object of study is clear from the beginning; it becomes so only gradually, as one passes to various levels of inquiry. Take, for example, the notion of literature which is in daily use, but is thorny as a mountain thistle. If in 1947 Sartre's question "What is literature?" seemed rather insidious, the question posed by Todorov at the first Congress of the I.A.S.S. (1974) was even more so: "Does literature exist?" Someone is actually casting doubt on the object, as if we were dealing with a collective ghost from which it would be opportune to liberate ourselves. Another critic, Zamjatin, who is also a writer, does not doubt the object but rather the possibility of describing it: there is an Indian fable, he says, in which "some blind people were asked to feel an elephant and describe what it seemed to them to resemble." One felt an ear and said: a rope. Another felt a hoof and said: a smooth column. A third felt the trunk and said: a sausage. Moral: "This is the destiny of the majority of critics. Literature is too vast a fact to be embraced in its totality" (Zamjatin, 1970, p. 41). Equally colorful but less rash is the reflection of Giorgio Manganelli: if only the great authors existed, literature would be a virgin forest in which dinosaurs roamed, but fortunately for literature, the great legion of minor writers exists and transforms the forest into a habitable place, well furnished, suitable for five o'clock tea.

The crisis in the area of definition has been described by the sociologist, Robert Escarpit: "There is nothing less clear than the concept of literature. The word itself is used in the most varied ways possible, and its semantic content is as rich as it is incoherent. In reality it is impossible to give a single, brief definition of literature" (in *Le littéraire et le social*, 1970, p. 13).

There are, besides, two opposing extremes: those theorists who consider literature as an intuitive act, and those who see it as the object of a perfect mechanism of rules. For the latter, literature is subject to an underlying system common to all the literatures of the world.

These examples, although extremely selective and concise, may serve to emphasize the fact that to take literature as an object of study is to proceed from something that is not—to begin with—at all evident. To have the intellectual certainty that it is evident, leads to the risk described by Proust in his famous phrase: *l'être devenu plus intelligent crée des droits à l'être moins.*

This having been said, the object of my study is the system of literature understood as the condition and the place of the literary communication that binds senders and addressees in various eras. That object will lead of necessity to an investigation of the notion of literature as a system with its own rules of functioning, rules conditioned from within and from without the system. It will lead also to an investigation of the notion of the text as a hypersign or polysemic message.

The inquirer who tends to search for systems is subject to alternating satisfactions and anxieties, if he remembers the insinuations of Borges that to want to remedy "the divine disorder of writing" is an aspiration no less empty than all other aspirations to order that men nourish. If a shared evil is already a part blessing, as the Italian saying has it, the researcher will make the best of a bad job and perhaps help himself out by turning to special *auctoritates,* those writers (poets above all) who have insistently asked themselves what the act of creation is, what the act of communication is, and who have attempted to answer those queries in pages that do enlighten us.

To set side by side the ideas of writers and those of semiologists and critics is the prerogative of this book and is an always profitable activity. It is also indispensable when, in facing the problem of the pre-text as an input of creative energy or of the generative structure of the text, one tries to understand if the need for communication is—from the beginning—a part of the deepest layer of the artistic process.

*Maria Corti*

An Introduction to Literary Semiotics

# I. Literature and Communication

## 1. LITERATURE AS SYSTEM

The first impression that any literature evokes, when considered in its entirety, is the image of a medieval *Wunderkammer*, where sheets of parchment lie next to embalmed animals, and magic stones adjoin alembics and painted panels. The various ways in which the imagination of a people has used writing result in an intricate, varicolored, and pluridirectional complex: lyrics, moral tracts, erotic texts, poems. A little of everything—just as in the universe—and, as in the universe, the directions seem infinite. But with further thought this impression can, like a double-faced garment, reverse itself at the moment in which the subtle rules of the game begin to surface: very little falls from the sky. Here is T.S. Eliot writing about literature in 1917:

> The existing monuments form an ideal order among themselves, which is modified by the introduction of the new (the really new) work of art among them. The existing order is complete before the new work arrives; for order to persist after the supervention of novelty, the *whole* existing order must be, if ever so slightly, altered; and so the relations, proportions, values of each work of art toward the whole are readjusted. . . .[1]

1

Thus, for Eliot, literature is not the sum of its texts but a kind of totality both linked and linking, and in movement: Eliot arrives at the concept of system. Postponing to sections 3 and 4 of this chapter the fundamental question of external links which arise from the sociocultural and ideological context of a period and from the dialectic between the system and the work, one can begin to focus on the notion of system. According to Eliot, artists always intuit, beneath the fluidity of the surface, the solidity of the literary context in which they are working. To this one must add that in periods in which the system is relatively stable there is no lack of evidence in the significant writers of irritation with and denunciation of that solidity; while in periods—like ours—of crises in ideological and therefore literary values, the system itself can be attacked as an arbitrary mechanism and its codes may be seen as mystifications (see IIIa.6; V.3). That is, the crisis of literature as a system is symptomatic of a crisis born elsewhere. If one adds to Eliot's observation Genette's penetrating idea,[2] one perceives that every valid work brings changes in the total literature precisely because, before its appearance, the system was "without gaps." Genette, even as he rejects the simplification implicit in his own simile, affirms that "the 'consumption' of literature by society is a *language*, or rather an ensemble, whose elements, whatever their number or nature, tend to organize themselves into a coherent system"; precisely because of that coherence, the expansion of literature is not the result of a filling in of lacunae.

The fact that literature is subject to structuring on various planes and levels seems to me fundamental to the notion of a literary system. Some of these levels are implicit in the diachronic development and the synchronic articulation of a literature, resulting from the interaction of its institutional forms and genres (see Chap. V) and the subtle relations that exist among literary phenomena. Other levels of structuring, superimposed on the first, have their genesis in the relation between a writer in his role as observer and the whole of a literature: the individual author draws on his favorite texts from the most varied and unpredictable literary places and times; he effects connections and interrelations among these favorite texts in relation to the constitutive law of his own work. Within the literary system, he creates the subsystem of his own sources. This phenomenon goes well beyond what Kristeva calls *l'intertextualité* or *les livres dans le livre*,[3] because it offers us a structural model of system that can function for a single work or for a writer's macrocosm or for the work of a literary group (for example, the "Petrarchans" of the early seventeenth century). From this perspective the traditional practice of analyzing sources takes on a new pertinence. That the ensemble of sources of an author or a literary group form a subsystem is proven by the fact that the eventual insertion of an "eccentric" source causes a split or a sudden transformation in the transsentential ambience of the text.[4]

There are still other ways of establishing levels susceptible of structuring. Perhaps most suggestive is the one wonderfully illustrated by Borges: "The fact is that each writer creates his precursors. His work modifies our conception of the past, as it will modify the future. In this correlation the identity or the plurality of men has no importance."[5] No longer is one speaking of literary links that, as in the case of sources, overlook the text, "surmounting" it, but rather of valleys; and Borges' declaration that the cause comes after the effect, even though it belongs in the list of his precious paradoxes, is absolutely valid in that every great work creates unforeseen links not only with the literature of the future, but with the literature of the past, thus transforming the sign value of earlier texts. Gianfranco Contini can therefore speak of the eternal Gadda function in Italian literature, and in light of Gadda we can discover an expressionistic canon from the thirteenth century to the present.

The quality of literature as a system can also be understood if we follow the diachronic movement of certain literary elements that Avalle calls "macrosigns,"[6] which appear with their own cluster of constants: legendary characters, motifs or topoi of thematic origin (the golden age, the amorous triangle, etc.). In the process of concretizing and actualizing these macrosigns, texts of different eras are involved in the combinatorial play of codified constants and textual variants.

The degree of cohesion and organization changes, obviously, from period to period; it is directly proportional to the faith that a given culture has in its literary institutions and it is inversely proportional to the writer's slipping away from his traditional confines and, even, from verbal confines. Typical in this sense in our age are visual poetry, scenography, the film script, comics (one thinks of Buzzati), the video-cassette, etc. A unified description of the whole is, for now, hardly possible. Germane to this account of literature is the definition of system offered by Gadda in his *Meditazione milanese:*

> We therefore think of every system as an infinite entwining, an inextricable knot or mesh of relations: the summit can be seen from many altitudes; and every system is referable to infinite coordinated axes: it presents itself in infinite ways.[7]

Such a conception, which is at once organic and dynamic, is well adapted both to catch the structural changes of literature from one era to another, and to individuate, through that which changes, that which does not change. Therefore, the specificity of a literature depends on the existence of special and unalterable relations—often intricate—among literary phenomena.[8]

## 2. INFORMATION AND COMMUNICATION SYSTEM

Consequently, it seems necessary to establish the types of relations, connections, and dependencies that are set up among texts and to indicate precisely the effective process by which individual messages are linked to the codifications of the system (Chap. V). We can follow the way inaugurated by the Russian Formalists, without forgetting, however, that the real task is not so much to discover the links and laws of structure (after all, structures can be discovered among all things in this world) or to find the general properties of literature, since one can find general properties for everything (and our culture has a rage for the general), but rather to test the functionality of such links and laws in light of the fact that literature is in itself a sign-information system. In other words, I do not intend to propose a way that leads to a science of the literary system as opposed to an inquiry into historical processes,[9] but rather to search for the skein that leads behind those phenomena that connote the sign system. Through and beyond the texts, that system produces information: disruptive acts of violence, disjunctive adventures, restructurings, the re-creation of a system of expectations, and recuperations (culture, we know, is repetitive); in sum, dynamic structures. Such an idea of literature acquires heuristic value in relation to the semiological study of the texts that compose the literature; and the texts are thus inserted into a semiotic circuit.

In this way, one arrives as well at the perception of literature as a *conditio sine qua non* of literary communication: the hypersign function of the literary text is fully realized in the general communicative process made possible by the existence of literary conventions and codifications (behind which stand the socioideological codes), by recognized techniques, which facilitate in some way the dialogue between author and addressee. Some of the principles which regulate such communication will be the object of several chapters of this book: for the moment it is enough to insist that the more artistically complex and original a work of art, the higher it rises over the works that surround it, the greater is its availability to different readings on both the synchronic and diachronic levels. Or rather, that quality of presence, that sense of perennial contemporaneity and universality produced by a masterpiece, results from the fact that the polysemic weight of the text allows it to be "used" in function of the literary—and, above all, the socio-ideological—models of various eras. Every era applies its own reading codes, its changed vantage points; the text continues to accumulate sign possibilities which are communicative precisely because the text is inside a system in movement. For equal and opposite reasons, the texts of minor writers and even more, of those who in all times make professional use of literature with a labored passivity, are less decodable as they move away from the system that first produced them. For example, for many Petrarchans of the second half of the fifteenth century, only the rules of the game, that is, of the strongly codified genre, reduce or eliminate gratuitousness and superinertia from the text, illuminating that literary operation which Gadda calls "a making out of the already made,"[10] or a secondary message.

To temporal distance one can add spatial distance. If today, a reader, equipped with a solid mastery of the Chinese language, were to encounter the poems that Su Huei, a noblewoman of the eastern Chin dynasty (317–420 B.C.), addressed to her warrior husband Tou T'ao, he would find fascinating poetic fragments, ambiguous and exotic, but the subtle message of the texts would be beyond him; he would lack the conventions and codes with which to read them. As Gustav and Innes Herdan have shown in their essay "Una struttura a fuga della poesia cinese classica" (A Fugal Structure in Classic Chinese Poetry) (*Strumenti Critici*, 6, 1968, pp. 233–240), the newness of this kind of poetry consisted in the application of the so-called "mechanism of the game of language," in which, starting from an original poem, one shifts the columns and inverts the ideograms inside a column on the basis of a formal mathematical device in order to produce a transformation of the text into its allotrope. In this case, which Lotman would place among the examples of the "semantic of many steps" (see here, IV. 4), before literary communication occurs, the addressee must not only be familiar with the conventions, codes and rules of the system, but with those texts of which the new messages are the allotropes, the partial heirs of older sign functions.

To conclude, at the basis of even the most original forms of literary communication there is an area of competence common to both the sender and addressee constituted by literature as an information and communication system.

## 3. FIELD OF TENSIONS; THE PLACE OF THE WORK

I have spoken (I.2) of the dynamic of structure: that is, of literature as a *field of tensions,* of centripetal and centrifugal forces produced in the dialectical relation between that which aspires to remain intact by inertia and that which advances with the force of rupture and transformation; where there is differentiation there is tension, therefore movement. At its limits, the work of highest originality seems to set itself outside the system like a happy alternative; but actually everything that precedes it is there, not only like the landscape in which one constructs a new building, but as a component of the collective consciousness and of the process through which the work will be "used." And then there is that which comes after the work: every masterpiece produces specific norms or particular links which will live autonomously, with respect to the text, in the work of imitators—norms and links that will perhaps be codified.[11]

The tensions are pluridirectional, as in all human sociocultural systems. A youthful literary movement tends to reach its majority and, vice versa (as Shklovsky shows), an artistic current produced by a new generation can also be reflected in the later work of the older generation; the models offered by the young can be imitated by the no longer young—an interlinking of the diachronic and synchronic analogous to that illustrated by Jakobson in linguistics.

The notions of literature as system and as field of tensions come together: to the first is linked the idea that every text has *a place* in the literature, in that it enters into a network of relations with the other texts; to the second, the idea that the place of a text is changeable, and may even be losable. And here it is important to refer to the extraliterary, to the sociocultural context, to which we shall soon return (I.4). The degree of conservation and changeability of the place of a work in the system is conditioned by many factors: there are long periods in which, as Koehler would say, "the seismograph of literature only registers minimal oscillations," when the movements of society itself are rather slow and its hierarchy of powers and values relatively stable.[12] In addition, there is the fact that the place of a work can be maintained, or even transformed and canonized, by conventions extraneous to the literary system, as happens to all models and cultural stereotypes imposed by a long, and often notorious, educational tradition that the power centers would like to perpetuate.

Because of the existence of a field of tensions, every text is subject to changing position diachronically in the intertextual network and—at the limit—to losing its position. On the diachronic level this phenomenon is joined to a double dynamic. On the one hand, a single text or series of texts or a whole literary genre is eclipsed, is assimilated into the fleeting stuff of time; the sociocultural context has been so transformed that the works have lost their hold on the thoughts and ideologies of classes, on the structures of the society and, finally, on the collective memory. It is important to observe how, in this case, the mediation of the literary system between the work and society is always relevant: the text tends more frequently to change or to lose its place in the sun in relation to the fate of the literary genre to which it belongs. On the other hand, there exist what Schücking calls the "phases of the moon" of popularity,[13] the rescuing of certain works distant in time for specific reasons, among which are the repetitive nature of sociocultural situations and phenomena.

Just as in the stock market, quotations rise or fall, so too there are stocks that disappear definitively from the literary market. For Blanchot, the situation taken all in all is not bleak:

One can say that the more a work is appreciated, the more it is in danger; it becomes a good work, it is arrayed on the side of the good, which exploits it, which makes of it a useful work. The work judged bad finds in this judgment the space in which it is often preserved. Set aside, relegated to the inferno by the libraries, burned, forgotten; but this exile, this disappearance into the heat of the fire or the tepidness of oblivion, prolongs in a certain way the just distance of the work, it corresponds to the strength of its having been set aside. . . . The work does not endure, it is [1955, p. 270].

In a different dialectical perspective, a ruthlessly ideological one, the loss of its place by a work is equal to the absolute loss of its worth as *merchandise*, which is the fate of the work in the consumer market; hence the ideal of the museum and the struggle against communication insofar as it makes merchandise out of works (see Sanguineti and the ideology of the neoavant-garde; see also Jameson, 1971, p. 395).

The sociologists of literature, remaining inside the rules of the game of history, not only see things differently but attempt to assemble catalogues and statistics of works that have disappeared definitively, leaving only notices of their existence; the result is vertiginous statistics.[14] As sociologists rightly maintain, there is a historic image of literature that has developed gradually at an elite level and to which every generation adds its own candidates, with the result that a significant number of authors and texts fall into a ghostly phase and then disappear like phantoms in the dark. The phenomenon of perishability is undoubtedly more tangible in other artistic systems: a Baroque portal substituted for a Romanesque, Byzantine frescoes covered by later Renaissance ones, etc. It is to be hoped in this regard that there will be further studies on the processes of artistic popularity—and its opposite—of the type conducted in France at the École Pratique des Hautes Études.[15]

The ideas of system and field of tensions can also lead to further reflections. Under the aegis of system one can examine the possibility of a future description and classification of literary institutions or genres, of large motifs or topoi, with their specific traits and, finally, of a typology of historically existent texts. Without the above-mentioned methodological premise, that is, without the principle of implication, the typology would end up as a simple inventory instead of offering something that resembles a paradigmatic structure—naturally on several levels—for a whole literature. In its turn, the concept of a field of tension, which introduces a dynamic vision of the system, proposes a typological model that does not impose a static image on literature. Jakobson's assertion that the synchronic is not the same as the static, while there does exist a "stasis of the diachronic," is always worth considering. One thinks, analogously, of the force of inertia in certain sectors of literature where one can individuate fossil-texts as against the inherent fluidity of other sectors.

## 4. THE SOCIOLOGICAL APPROACH

Obviously, literature is never an antiseptic lodging place for literary products; such a perception would be the result of looking at literature too close up, of losing sight of part of its reality. Literature is not an acropolis, nor even a walled city. The Russian Formalists of the Thirties and, in their wake, the semiologists of the Prague School (Mukařovský) and the current School of Tartu, have all shown how society, in its relation to literature, seems like a rich cluster of sociocultural, economic and ideological directions that, with more or less intensity, influence the literary system because they form part of the collective consciousness.

The sociology of literature and sociological criticism[16] have resulted from this reflection on literature as a social phenomenon. Recently Corsini, even though he adheres to a well-known current of ideological criticism, has insisted on the fact that the central core of the question is unresolved and leads to problems that offer little consolation. We have first to inquire into the role of the institution that regulates the vital possibilities of the author-text-reader circuit. Only thus can we establish "the conditions under which the mechanism of production and of use of the so-called artistic or literary product functions."[17] In other words, in the societies that we encounter in history, the monopoly of the use or even of the manipulation of cultural goods belongs to the class or classes that hold power; their cultural influence must be deciphered not only as an instance of conspiratorial consensus, but as the result of nearly infrangible prohibitions which lie at the origins of cultural codes themselves. The status of a culture is also cumulative and—at times, overarching temporal distance—even repetitive; and this is a historically justified phenomenon. But the officially recognized culture tends to be conservative or narcissistic, that is, to impose the past as the model for the present, well beyond that justifiable point.

Clearly, an investigation of this nature concerns sociology *tout court,* or the science of all social phenomena, including the literary. In this perspective, literary works are not more valuable because they are literary; they are of value only for their testimony as documents of a socioideological process, of the social dynamic or the social stasis of culture in general (for the semiological consequences of this problem as applied to literature, cf. here I.5).

Sociological inquiry today exists on different levels—depending on whether it deals with artistic creation itself (sociological criticism) or with production for a market and use (a sociology of artistic communication, where communication has a more restricted sense than the one I am using). One can add to these inquiries sociopoetics, theoretical in nature, which concerns itself with problems of the general theory of the relations between literary and social structures.[18]

In the area of sociological criticism, research tends to center on the following question: do strict ties exist between socioeconomic and literary structures and, if so, on what level and with what instruments is it possible to nail down the homology concretely, to individuate the structural correspondences? Some researchers operate on a strictly theoretical level, concentrating on the "conceptualization" of structural relations between society and literature, society and work (for example,

C. Bouazis), following Goldmann's line of "genetic structuralism" and refusing a simplistic relation between social contents and the contents of the work. According to Goldmann and his heirs, the writer, belonging to a specific social group, carries to an advanced level of coherence the rudimentary structures elaborated by the group or—better—the *processus de structuration* of the group; so that the work comes to represent, through the activity of an individual awareness, a collective awareness.[19] The task of sociological criticism, according to Goldmann, is difficult: it is intent on individuating the homologies between the processes of a more or less compact collective awareness and those of an individual awareness— but the latter is rather less delimitable because of the many ambiguities in the artistic process. The major complication is the fact that every structure is in its turn insertable into greater, more encompassing, structures.[20] It seems to me that a positive contribution of Goldmann's thought is the relation he establishes between the genesis of a work and its structure. He is also attentive to the reality of a work of art—and does not share the imperious disinterest of some sociologists for the particular nature of the object with which they are dealing. However, the question of the homology of structures remains very problematic.

Koehler had already shown how it would be somewhat ingenuous to suppose that changes in the infrastructure automatically produce new forms and content, for that can occur only during moments that are marked by revolution. But even then, this effect is more evident in the case of literary genres— that is, the larger structures of the system—than in single works, especially since "up until the French Revolution the borders between genres and styles have coincided with class differences."[21] That the relation between social structures and structures of the literary system or literary genres is easier and more profitably investigated than the relation between social structures and the single work, is a reality which one must bear in mind: the mediation of literary institutions (for instance, genres) is of primary importance and adds a confirmation to the fact that the literary system is an information system. In the same historical-social context, literature offers a proliferation of genres that often are destined for different social strata: that Boiardo uses a profoundly different mode of writing when he adheres to the institution of the lyric from that which he uses when writing a chivalric poem is both cause and effect of the different publics to which the two genres are addressed. The corollary of this is that the various social strata read the works of a given genre differently (for a treatment in greater depth of this problem, cf. Chap. V, devoted to literary genres). Therefore, processes of a conservative nature on the socioideological level condition the types of relations and the modes of transformations within the literary system. In this regard, what has been happening in these last years is most significant. Literary genres, which are in crisis in literature at its highest level, have passed into the mass media, where genre conventions have indeed been strengthened: television novels, historical or not, romantic novels in popular magazines, detective stories, novellas in tabloids, etc. (cf. V. 3). This operation, carried out by the dominant class, is ultraconservative and reactionary; it is the product of a power that hinders with all its means the actualization of that program of proletarian literature formulated for the first time in Russia in 1918 and reproposed in various moments and places on a Marxist-Leninist base.[22]

But the question of connections between social structures and individual works is a more difficult one to confront or resolve.[23] Koehler, in the article cited, has already observed that for the "extensive totality" of the real and the social, the single work substitutes the "intensive totality" of its esthetic coherence, arrived at through a selective and selecting activity with respect to the real. But many other obstacles interpose themselves between the ardent hunter of homologies and the homologies themselves: the existence of inverted relations and projections between the work and society; the flight into the imaginary as compensation (here, see the sociology of the imaginary in Duvignaud and, from another vantage point, psychoanalytic criticism); the processes of contradiction between the work and its author, between the work and the real—not to mention all the disjunctions generated by the position of the writer who announces, anticipates the future or creates emblems of utopia, or the writer who willfully looks backwards. To this one can add the obstacles imposed by the very nature of the literary work, which can never be considered within the frame of pure synchrony, since it inherits and channels traditional motifs and stereotypes. The only thing that is evident in a work is its ambiguous complication.

In this still completely open field it will be more useful to proceed at the pace of microsociology,[24] with the long patience of repeated inspections, without forgetting that a work of fantasy often reveals its social conditioning more than does a so-called realistic work, organized in a mimesis of the real. In this regard Rossi-Landi writes,

> We shall say therefore that we have a form of *artistic realism* every time the artist or writer *codifies a message destined* (in that market of language and communication, that is, in that society and in that historic moment) *to be decoded* by the public *as representative of the dominant ideology.* And we would add that since in every highly organized situation there is little choice, the artistically realistic message is distinguished from other artistic messages by a *relatively low quantity of information.*[25]

If, as the sociologists themselves affirm, up until today the problematic and empirically experimental phase remains dominant over the definitive and locally resolved, then perhaps the assertion of Jacques Dubois would be of interest to us. He suggests that a transversal analysis, that is, one carried out on a group or on several groups of literary texts, even of different genres, is more revealing than a direct approach to a single text, since

> through dissection, classification and enumeration one is really rending the veil that hides the network of relations at the base of the text and allowing us to make more precise the influence of

crude elements and, above all, the influence of another order of relations. This second order, once individuated, can probably be shown to rest on the laws of the collective unconscious which leave their traces on the work and allow us to perceive the most socialized aspect of the message.[26]

It is the ensemble of a literature, therefore, that allows the aspect of the message that is most socialized to be emphasized. Consequently, sociological critics find themselves having to confront an analysis of the literary forms and contents of a given era in function of specific milieus, of behavioral factors, and of the values that are dominant or rejected in a given class context, and, more generally, in function of the structures and superstructures of a society: at the same time these critics must be attentive to the complex fact that the same ethicocultural models can stand behind works that are vastly different among themselves. For this, see the analysis of Zalamansky or the earlier work of Albrecht[27] (and see also IIb.)

The so-called sociology of communication offers a vast panorama of empirical research, devoted to the phenomena of production (type, frequency, and volume of production) and of consumption (ambience, kind, and volume of use).[28] The researches of Escarpit into the economic, political, social, and pedagogical aspects of consumption are well known, as are the investigations of Mury and the group of the Bordeaux school with its Centre de Sociologie des Faits Littéraires directed by Escarpit, and the group in Lièges. The replacement of the *text* by the *literary fact* is significant: what is of interest to these sociologists of literature is the circle of communication and not the content of that communication, the contact between producer and consumer, not the entity of the message.[29]

Undeniably something of the rough and rustic remains at the root of these collections, systemizations and typologies of the flowers of literature for consumption only: infusions, lotions, pomades, and even photograph albums; it would seem that it is a price the sociologists are willing to pay in order to make of the sociology of literature a science.

I have noted in the Foreword that the point of view from which one considers an object makes pertinent certain kinds of inquiries and not others; the critic's activity is selective. For that reason I am excluding from this work that type of inquiry which, even though it begins with literature, soon leads to a discourse which is alternative or complementary to literature itself; that is, to strictly sociopolitical and ideological inquiry that is based not on an examination of textual complexity, but on content-centered paraphrases of the text as a reflection of ideology.[30]

## 5. THE SEMIOLOGICAL APPROACH

At this point the semiological approach presents itself not only with profit but with stimulating vigor. Mukařovský, even across the distance of years, still speaks with limpid *auctoritas:*

> Without a semiological direction the theorist will always tend to consider the work of art as a purely formal construction, or as a direct reflection of the psychological or even physiological disposition of the author, either in the distinct reality expressed by the work, or in the ideological, economic, social or cultural situations of a given environment. This will lead the theorist to treat the developmental process of art as a sequence of formal transformations or to ignore the developmental process (as do some current schools of psychological esthetics), or to conceive it as a passive reflection of a process external to art. Only the semiological point of view will allow theoreticians to recognize the autonomous existence and the essential dynamism of the structure of art and to understand its evolution as an immanent movement, but in a relationship in constant dialectic with the evolution of other fields of culture.[31]

According to Mukařovský, therefore, a semiological conception of literature has the advantage of creating a network of relations between the signs of the literary series and those of other series, thus avoiding a unilateral approach to texts as pure literary objects or as direct witnesses of a reality which is external to them.

A fruitful point of departure is the collective consciousness, with its unconscious and conscious components, of which the sociocultural and ideological series are expressions. The first task is to show the type of signedness or sign-quality in which this collective consciousness is expressed in every era, and the level of signedness, which can be major or minor according to how symbolic is the culture being studied.[32] The Middle Ages, for example, is a period of highly symbolic—what Auerbach would call "figural"—culture.[33] The first example that comes to mind, for the evidence of its figural phenomena, is that of the bestiaries, in which existent animals such as the rooster and absolutely fantastic animals such as the unicorn can exist on the same plane without the surprise or unease of the public, since their cultural reality is exquisitely signlike. In the bestiaries, animals symbolize the virtues and vices: whether these animals existed in the barnyard or have never been seen on land or sea is completely secondary to the sender of the message and to the addressees.

Of greater importance is the fact that to the sign-types of a period belong its social models; thus Lotman, illustrating—in the article cited above—the model of medieval society, emphasizes the particular rapport between individual and group, that is, between the part and the whole; man, independently of his existential reality, counts socially in that he is part of a group and as such also has the function of representing that group, of serving as its sign: "The real existence of the human being depended on his relation with the structure of which he was a sign" (Lotman, p. 46). Thus, a social model with a high sign-function is mirrored in the literary system.

It seems to me that there is highly suggestive material in the work of the Dominican Umberto da Romans, *De eruditione praedicatorum*, in two volumes, of which the second belongs to the genre of *sermones ad status*, sermons addressed to specific social groups, common in the twelfth and thirteenth centuries.[34] In Umberto da Romans' work the remote scene of medieval society is represented so that each social group has its own *status*, its own place in a hierarchy, in a "construction that is shown to be unitary and connected internally by a series of relations of ever-larger inclusiveness. For example, the *maiores civitatis* belong to the larger category of the *laici in civitatibus,* then to the still larger category of *laici,* then to the *Populus Christianus,* then to the *Omnes homines.*"[35] Let us add an example from the ecclesiastical realm: one starts from the Templars or from the *Fratres teutonici,* to rise from the *status* of the group to that of the superior unities: *Religiosi arma portantes,* then *Omnes religiosi* (that is, members of a religious order), then to *Omnes personae ecclesiasticae,* then *Populus Christianus*—in contradistinction to the *Infideles*—and, finally, *Omnes homines.*

The hierarchic social model of more-embracing inclusiveness is reflected both in the organization of literary institutions and in individual works. Umberto, who follows the literary genre of the *Sermones,* knows that he cannot offer general preaching models but only *sermones ad status:* every individual, every soul to be carried to heaven, finds his reality and his sign-function inside the group structure with its specific *status.* As evidence of the type of signedness in which the medieval collective consciousness is expressed, not only is the social series linked to the literary series, but some of the principles that regulate literary communication are made clear, such as the sign-function of that communication and the manner in which communication links senders and addressees of the artistic message.

We can move up one more step: the type of signedness characteristic of a period produces that period's so-called "world view." Look now—in this perspective—at the *De vulgari eloquentia* of Dante, where the author, in his treatment of the "illustrious" use of the vulgar tongue in its relation to regional versions, takes as his starting point Adam and the questions posed by the Scholastics: who spoke first, what did he say, to whom, where, when. That is, even a man as attentive to the quotidian and as sublimely curious about the existential as was Dante, is nevertheless convinced that the problem of language is real insofar as it is seen as universal and symbolic; he cannot help but insert his linguistic discourse into a type of pyramidal modeling of reality that rests on the creative act of the word itself as sign, on the divine meaning of the first verbal sign (*El*

= God in Hebrew), and on the fact that such a human verbal sign is a response to the nonverbal, but highly communicative, signs, expressed by God through nature. The open circle at the beginning of the *De vulgari eloquentia* will be closed when the "illustrious" vulgar tongue is seen as a model which, like the Adamic model, has a high sign-power: both of these models are, for Dante, natural models—the Adamic model given by God and the "illustrious" vulgar tongue by Poetry.

Inside every historical sign system there exists a hierarchy of cultural codifications well-known to the sender and to the addressee of a message, what one might call the syntax of these codes. The important thing is to be aware that syntax is never neutral, it is ideologized.[36] The destruction of the level of signedness of a period, that is, the desemiotization of a cultural system, leads necessarily, as Lotman has demonstrated, to a new and different type of semiotization, and therefore of communication. In fact, Gombrich, following Ernest Jones, sees the process of transformation in the world of the arts as a continual unmasking of the preceding symbols, for which new ones are substituted.[37]

In this light, the literary work offers a double testament of itself; the artist, on the one hand, has the rigorous destiny of ingathering the deep, indecipherable obscurity of the real and, on the other, of connecting in a new way the signs emitted by the referents in the cultural and ideological world of his own age—a process through which he participates in the social nature of literary structures. He is conditioned by that social nature whether he favors the system of expectations of that society or whether he places himself in opposition to it (see IIb.5). Literature then appears as a place for the meeting or collision of the individual and collective consciousnesses, an encounter that changes with the changes of history: if today the attitude of collision predominates in the writer (see IIa.6), in an age like the medieval the writer, facing a series of codes and preset hierarchical orders, did not feel curbed in his freedom. Originality, in fact, does not depend on the dogma of originality, a dogma of Romantic origin.

# II. Sender and Addressee

## A. *The Sender*

### 1. SELF-COMMUNICATION

There are textual situations in which the sender of the message is identical with the addressee, so that the text assumes the character of self-communication.[1] One conspicuous example is the 1954 *Diario* of Beppe Fenoglio, a series of brief remarks that the author wrote solely for himself. For this reason he made use of abbreviations with indexical value, and of a sequence of notes which serve several functions: to register and to preserve something for future memory or to pin down associative processes that accumulate in the writer's mind and await organization. Whatever its purpose, the information is entrusted to time and not to space. It inhabits an individual territory—Fenoglio's—and its transcription can be as instrumental as is the everyday use of language, regardless of the fact that, in our later reading, the language may seem so artistic as to presuppose an author-function.

There are cases, as in Stendhal's personal notes in his manuscripts, in which self-communication makes use of cryptographic procedures, privileged evidence for any psychoanalytic perspective on intersubjectivity (cf. IIa.3). However, if what Proust says is true, and the "permanent I, which extends throughout the entire duration of our life" is made up of "all our successive I's that, in sum, constitute it [the permanent I] in

20

part,"[2] one objective of textual self-messages is communication among these successive "I's," out of our desire to escape from the cancellations in memory of unrepeatable moments, from the fruit of the lotus, from a breakdown of internal continuity.

A qualitatively different phenomenon—though it too wears the guise of self-communication—occurs when the sender, having become the reader of his own work, becomes to some degree part of the series of addressees; this occurs when the author discovers a break between the text and the personal experience that generated it. It is the final aspect of the author-work relationship, very different in nature from the self-communication to which we first referred.

## 2. EXTRATEXTUAL INDICES

The sender of the artistic message is present in the double role of real person or historical individual and implied author—to use the terminology of Wayne Booth in *The Rhetoric of Fiction*[3]—or constructor of the work. In general, biographical research, in itself relevant, is extraneous to the immanent study of the text, if what Blanchot says of the author is true: "And the work finally ignores him, it closes itself in his absence, in an impersonal, anonymous affirmation, and nothing more."[4] In reality, however, things are more complex; first, a real problematic may exist in the relation between the sender as a historical person and the structural laws of the work. An author's life does not unwind like a ball of thread; life events occur and moments of a particular vital condensation intervene, in the flux of events, with distinctive features and traits in contrast to other features pertinent in other periods of the writer's life. Distinctive biographical aspects are functional for a work when they contribute to its structuring; in such happy cases a special kind of meeting of the author with a chain of signs emitted by the referents is at the root not only of the work but of its particular organization. For this reason an analysis of the structure of the text itself and a recognition of extratextual indices become complementary—rather than contradictory—procedures.

The fact that in the past the extratextual, biographical method has been overemphasized must not lead us now to the analogous excess of a purely immanent study of the text.

Elsewhere, I have furnished examples from the work of Elio Vittorini that, seen from this viewpoint, are suggestive and illuminating.[5] Here one can cite the *Ur Partigiano Johnny* by Beppe Fenoglio, a text written entirely in English, out of which came two works published together as *Partigiano Johnny.* Both the thematic frame—with its precise chronology indicated not only in months but days—and the stylistic register can be explained only by reference to extratextual factors: from the documents on partisan Fenoglio in the Ministry of Defense,[6] it turns out that Fenoglio, from March 1, 1945, to the Liberation, had been assigned by the Partisan Command to the English mission then operating in Piedmont. Not only does the work have the same chronological boundaries as the events lived by its author, but on a structural level it offers a relation of absolute identification between the implied author and the work's protagonist. This absolute relation is extraneous to Fenoglio's other work; here it is motivated by the psychological pressure of a vivid, specific experience. Not only the thematic structure but also the linguistic style (the use of a highly personal lyrical English) has its motivation in autobiography, that is, in the first emotional encounter of Fenoglio with the Anglo-Saxon world in flesh and blood and uniforms—that privileged world which he had mythologized since his adolescence. In other words, when homologies between textual and extratextual structures do exist, they must be dealt with whatever one's critical approach; to overlook them is to diminish the text, in Gadda's image, to "a parcel post package," to "a *gnocco* [singular of *gnocchi*] detached from others in the pot," to a text that is referred back (Gadda is still speaking) "to something other, to something other, infinitely to something other."[7]

Besides the problem of specific biographical traits that influence the structure of the work, there is the less subtle but more general problem of the situation in which the sender of the message was implicated and to which he refers in the work. Just as, in ordinary discourse, the situation semantically frames the enunciation and becomes a unit of analysis with a functional value, so is the recognition of a situation index, often biographical in nature, indispensable for the critical comprehension of the literary message. Important in this regard is the examination by Mounin of the poetic text *Toilette* by Eluard, that is, a type of writing which, by its nature, is much more independent of the universe of referents than are other types of poetry, or even more so, prose.[8] An ignorance of the situation to which Eluard alludes has led to some ten different readings, none of them attributable to the polysemy of the text, but to a selection of the wrong situational indices; as a result of this, the various readings produce not enrichment but a lessening of the message. It should be noted that I do not wish to exclude the possibility that infinite readings of a text by its readers can lead, in the varied combinatorial games of language, to a new text, to a message that was ignored by the author but is equally valid; such a possibility belongs "naturally," according to Montale, to the life of poetry, not to the author-message relation. Foucault suggests that the need for such a relation-operation explains the instinctive unease that a reader experiences when the writer of a work is unknown and is accepted only as an enigma, as something that needs resolution philologically—at least in our cultural context, though certainly not in all others, as the Middle Ages demonstrate.[9]

## 3. THE IMPLIED AUTHOR

A consideration of the sender leads to the concept of the implied author or *constructor* of the work: events, emotions, private illuminations are transformed into artistic procedures from which the notion of an implied author is the only deduction. And yet Chatman, following Wayne Booth, observes that whenever the implied author is present as "official scribe" or *alter ego* of the author, it is clear that "however impersonal he tries to be, his reader will inevitably construct an image of the official scribe who writes in that manner—and naturally that official scribe will not be neutral about all values."[10] Todorov says the same thing: "There exists another *I*, an *I* most often invisible, which refers to the narrator, that 'poetic personality' that we seize through the discourse."[11] The grip of this invisible "I" is conveyed by Borges in a humorous remark: there are authors of the past and the present to whom the reader, after his having read them, would have an instinctive desire to telephone and others for whom this desire would never arise. In the reflections of the text this omnipresent phantom *becomes* the author-function to which Foucault links the actual typology of discourses: "Briefly, it is a question of detaching from the subject (or from the substitute therefore) his role as the original foundation, and analyzing him as a variable and complex function of the argument."[12] Thus, such a typology will include the various relations between the "I" of the narrator or subject of the enunciation and the "I" and the "him" of the explicit person or persons, subjects of the enunciated (relations which have already been the objects of several studies—those of Todorov, Kristeva, Chatman, and Rousset).

However, the critics' work is complicated by the presence of the intersubjectivity of the author—of the unconscious with its specific logic and of the conscious—interrelated in the message in a more or less coherent and commensurate manner. This explains why psychoanalytic criticism contains such diverse ways of approaching the question of the sender-text or lifework relation. Starobinski's penetrating study of the relation between psychoanalysis and literature[13] makes clear at least one fundamental dichotomy. On the one hand, there are those who see no break in continuity between the "interior history that precedes the work" and the work itself seen as "an act of desire, an intention made manifest." What they maintain is not merely an analogy, but an active collaboration between the dream and the work of art. In this regard, Gramigna, in his recent book, has posed the question: "In what sense is dream an alternative writing? In the sense that one uses dream as an outlet for the practical incapacity of tracing words on paper, or in the sense that dream continues, according to a different linguistic code, the writings of our waking life?"[14] It is revealing that here the question is asked by a novelist.

On the other hand, there are those, like Starobinski himself, who claim that only the text, eloquent enough in itself, speaks. In addition, even a linguist like Jakobson, basing himself on the concept of the "autonomous discourse" of Khlebnikov, can (for his part) arrive at a perception of the presence of elements underlying the consciously orientated organization of linguistic materials, phonetic elements that become phonological in that they are subliminal structures.[15] The great reserve of poetic energy that belongs to the unconscious is actualized on the level of meanings hidden within the text and formal structures that act according to the principles of subjective saturation; these may be found text by text, but they are always such that they overdetermine the formal structures themselves.[16] The distinction between the artist who speaks and he who is spoken by the individual and collective unconscious resembles in a strange way a secular, and up to a certain point scientific, mode of reapplying the Pauline and Augustinian discourse of the man speaking by himself and of the man who is spoken by Grace.

The experience of literature can prompt our awareness of another type of relation: between the unconscious of the author—the absent text—and the present text. In at least one case this relation is clarified by an intermediate link in the chain. We have the rare and precious example of the boyhood writings of Leopardi from the years 1809–1810[17] which, even if they do not, save for a few exceptions, contain work of a high artistic level, are nevertheless meaningful testimony to a deep-structure system of poetic connections still in their embryonic state: the first manifestations of the poetic idiolect of the artist or of his individual language. These early writings prove that in the depths of an individual and, in a special way, of an artist, there exist empty formal structures that await their fulfillment; with Lacan we can call them "signifiers that take precedence over the signified."[18] The fulfillment of Leopardi's poetic idiolect is slow and progressive: the boy Leopardi has a premonition of his own future poetic signifiers, for example, certain rhythmic structures which are still unknown to him, that is, which he uses unconsciously. Thus the documentary importance of these youthful texts lies not only in their presentation of unconscious activity but in their allowing us to examine the signs of that predestined later poetic communication. Let us choose as an example the first prose of 1809—perhaps actually 1808[19]—which is undoubtedly a school exercise; it is a small theme entitled *Descrizione d'un incendio* (Description of a Fire) of only 36 lines. It is ingenuous in content and stylistically it has many Latinizing inversions and rhetorical figures—in other words, it is a work based on scholastic models. However, we read a little prose exercise and simultaneously we encounter the surprising rhythms of numerous hendecasyllables and *settenari*. [Our English partial analogue of the hendecasyllable is, of course, the pentameter, and of the *settenario*, the trimeter line. The coupling of hendecasyllable and *settenario* would find its analogue in two lines such as: But he who dreams of sleeping with his wife / lays claim to paradise. Also we find that particular form of hiatus or diaeresis—*dialefe*—in which the two successive vowels *not* to be elided are found at the end of one word and at the beginning of the next—in this example, the *a* of *da* and the *i* of *insolito*.—A.M.] The hendecasyllables are:

14, *ripeter voglia anche dal duro sasso*
16, *vedo là mucchi di annerite pietre*
19, *vedo un'afflitta donna, che seduta*
24, *vicino ad essa un vecchio scarmo stassi*
26, *anche un fanciullo, che non ben comprende*

The hendecasyllable with *dialefe*:

4, *mi desto da insolito stupore*

Couplings of a hendecasyllable and a *settenario*:

12—13, *stride la fiamma, e si raddoppia e gira*
      *in vortici frementi*
34—35, *per voi piange l'amico,*
      *e per voi di amarezza ha colmo il seno.*

Coupling of *settenari*:

1—2, *fra le squarciate nubi*
      *mostravasi di volo*

(images that will proliferate in a very different context, in *Cantica*, IV, 62: *fendersi vidi i nugoli e squarciarse*).

The endings of the phrases and sentences, always rhythmic, offer from the beginning a significant number of *settenari*:

3, *in tranquillo riposo*
12, *ed al suolo l'uguaglia*
18, *infocata scintilla*
23, *interrotto sospiro*
25, *tra la morte e l'affanno*
32, *Qual ti rivedo adesso!*
33, *la gioia ed il contento*
34, *l'affanno, ed il cordoglio*

All of the prose bears striking witness to this phenomenon: added to the rhythm of the sequences with constant repetition of hendecasyllables and *settenari* are the variable repetitions of other measures. As Jakobson has clearly illustrated,[20] the reiterative phonic figure is a procedure that belongs only to the poetic function of language, a function that the very young Leopardi possessed in its natural state. Two phenomena, characteristic and complementary, are present in the prose: (1) the Latinizing inversions resulting from the "execution" of prose models learned at school; (2) the frequent imbuing of these models with an unconscious poetic rhythm. It is as if the boy Leopardi does not recognize the aspects of verse form in his

rhythmic choices; he does not know he is writing verses,
neither has he any experience of poetic prose, and yet by in-
stinct he chooses the phonic-rhythmic structure capable of
endowing the words with suggestiveness: he gives to the structure that connotative function that Vinogradov called "the expressive aureole." That the procedure of inserting verses is unconscious is confirmed by two circumstances: its repeatability is
not organized according to rules of construction but follows the
course of the young Leopardi's emotions; in addition, two
years later when the rationalizing attitude takes over—within
the limits possible to a twelve year old, even of genius—
Leopardi purges the poetry from his prose writing (when his
first writings on logic, ethics, and metaphysics are born).

In turning to Leopardi's prose of 1809, a further advance is
made in those cases where the hendecasyllable of the prose has
a syntactic structure and a syntagm of a future verse of the
*Canti;* for example, the beginning of Prose III, a hendecasyllable
with *dialefe,* "*Nasce l'uomo adorno di ragione,*" cannot help but
recall the "*Nasce l'uomo a fatica*" from *Canto notturno di un pastore
errante nell'Asia.* In other prose specimens what strikes us is not
the presence of verses, but of a rhythmic-syntactic structure
produced with the prolepsis of an indirect complement, which
returns later in an identical way and with the same complement
in well-known verses (poetic syntax, we know, is a rhythmic
sense of proportions). In Prose V, 77–79, we read:

> La parca mensa è già terminata, e alla primiera fatica ciascuno lieto, e
> indefesso ritorna. Intanto il sole declina all'orizonte. . . .

The hendecasyllable "*ciascuno lieto, e indefesso ritorna*" with accents on the 4th and 7th syllable derives from the prolepsis of
the complement "*alla primiera fatica,*" just as in the *Sabato del
villaggio* the hendecasyllable with accents on the 2nd, 6th, and
10th

> 42, *ciascuno in suo pensier farà ritorno*

is produced by the anticipation of the complement "*al travaglio usato."* The example is reinforced by the thematic recurrence, obviously on different levels of writing: *"alla primiera fatica | al travaglio usato; ciascuno | ciascuno; ritorna | farà ritorno." "La parca mensa"* is the same styleme as verse 28 of *Sabato del villaggio: "E intanto riede alla sua parca mensa";* of which the *intanto* is present here as *"Intanto il sole declina all' orizonte,"* with its semantic-rhythmic force, while a supplementary situational encounter is offered by verse 2, *"In sul calar del sole."*

The first steps toward Leopardi's future syntactic-stylistic usages can be traced in his use of antitheses realized with an adversative clause introduced by *ma*, which generates a rhythmic counterattack:

> *La Spelonca, 5, Tutto riposa; ma riposo, o tregua*
> *Tirsi non trova . . .*

where the antithesis already bears the stamp of Leopardi; in fact there is an alliterative continuity; the dental of *tutto* and the liquid of *riposo* of the first line meet and are woven into *tregua, Tirsi,* and *trova* of the second line. This is certainly not consciously done (or the boy would have been a monster), but we are in fact in front of that phonic dissemination or dissemination of meanings that Agosti and Beccaria have illustrated in various poetic examples, construing those disseminations as informal messages. Agosti, in fact, has drawn his illustration from a text by Leopardi and refers to the "secret and truly biological irrationality of forms." This argument obviously goes well beyond the other approach in which both the boy Leopardi and the adult Leopardi are seen as having syntagms, stylemes, and syntactic structures in common because behind both the boy and the man there is the same tradition of poetic Italian language—the same sources. It goes beyond that for two reasons: (1) both Leopardis choose certain formal models and not others; the choice can assume, despite two very different levels of artistic maturity, the same direction (Tasso, Varano, et al.) because it is congenial; (2) the boy always takes over certain formal models when he is spurred on by certain themes; un-

consciously he responds more intensely to themes like sol-
itude, nature, night, or to storm as a physical opposite of nature's quiet—only then is the informal message that belongs to
Leopardi's poetic idiolect realized. Then he writes as he feels,
while in other cases he feels as he writes, that is, his true nature
sleeps in infancy.

Elsewhere I shall refer to other examples from Leopardi; here
I wanted to focus attention on a phase intermediary between
the absent text, that is, the artist's unconscious, and the texts
present in great poetry, by looking at the symbolic operation
through which juvenilia are already signals of future poetry. Or
to suggest a metaphoric meaning in the fine pages by Daniello
Bartoli entitled *Notomia del ventre d'un piccolissimo Seme a trovarvi
dentro tutto il Corpo d'un grandissimo Albero*[21]: attention, Bartoli
writes, to the great miracle by which the seed is miniscule
compared to that which will grow from it in time; one cannot
distinguish clearly the qualities that will later separate out;
what will later be organized now seems confused, and yet the
seed of a fir, an oak, a chestnut, a palm, a pine contains in its
apparent lack of distinction the distinctive traits of the future
tree.

Following a line indicated by Zanzotto in a prose commentary on his poem *Gli sguardi, i fatti e senhal,* I should like to refer
to another aspect of the relation between the unconscious of
the sender and the text, that of "induced psychic states." Zanzotto says that the text is closed but that it can begin again
circularly and one can "actually assist at a parade of these
phantoms—not even figurines, not even voices—variants of an
I that is not, and of a rather dubious unconscious, or perhaps
voices of psychic states induced as by drugs. Under the
influence of drugs a series of psychic states is induced that was
at first unthinkable: the same individual influenced by mes-
caline or by psilocybin or by *LSD self-produces* another psychic
state which no longer has a relation either with the gods or with
history. Yes, these are truly voices of induced psychic states,
voices that ask nothing and at the same time ask all and which

in their fragmentary nature announce, if nothing else, the pride of their occurrence, or their imposition as fact, as presences while *they are not.*"[22]

## 4. AREA OF COMPETENCE

For the author, the passage from the personal sphere to that of artistic execution cannot happen unless, as Eliot maintains,[23] there is a critical act, "the labour of sifting, combining, constructing, expunging, correcting, testing." I add a postscript: there are authors who might not be inherently greater than others but who become so because they know how to look at their own act of creation with the distance of the user, that is, of the reader. Particular exemplars of this are Poe, Baudelaire, Valéry (see IIIb).

But before the initial action of a strategy of construction, that is, before the concrete passage of the author to the side of his work, there exists an initial phase of the creative process that simultaneously involves the side of the author and that of the text. When Borges speaks of a drama of alternatives in which every choice of a plot, of a space, and of a narrative time always carries, for him who makes it, the renunciation of another plot, another space, another narrative time that present themselves to the mind and are equally inviting,[24] he is guiding us directly into the zone of the artist's so-called "competence." In general, the notion of competence is understood by the critic intuitively as is the notion of the text and, in general, such intuitions function well. However, the theorist of poetics or literature (Ihwe or Van Dijk can be cited here[25]) is interested in the competence of the artist in a very different way. For example, Van Dijk, who takes the generative approach to literary theory, starts from the notion of a basic scheme or deep structure that, through various transformations, produces the macrostructures of single texts; in narrative terms the *fabula* can be considered as the deep structure and the plot of the text its macrostructure. Such theories are interested in the problem of the competence of the sender not only with regard to existent texts but also to possible texts, that is, those not yet written, to the *type* rather than to the *token*, [26] which explains the search for general rules underlying the formation of literary texts.

Nevertheless, Borges, with his reference to the alternatives of the pre-textual phase, invites us to a reflection on the complexity of the problem of the productive competence of texts: that which is not chosen by the writer does not automatically undergo cancellation and can in some way equally influence the work in progress. The area of reflection on artistic competence is privileged on the writers' part; writers are the only ones to have a direct experience of the phenomenon. For example, Calvino in his *Castello dei destini incrociati* and especially in the section of the book called "Tutte le altre storie," offers a concrete and at the same time symbolic experiment concerning the way in which every *fabula* can be dismembered and recombined differently, so that every plot and consequently every story constructed from that plot is potentially interchangeable with others in the consciousness of its begetter.

The competence of the artist encounters a corresponding competence in the addressees, who can thus understand a plot and can even anticipate its outcome, especially in cultures or literary genres that are well codified. For this reason Escarpit can speak—even for the project-phase of a work—of a "game of four cantons" between the work as psychological event, content, form, and sociological event: "Before every attempt at expression, the work and consciousness of the writer already flow easily into each other. The project is their point of conscious intersection, and the sociological event predominates over the psychological event in the sense that before the project can be realized, the writer must structure it dialectically at the levels of expression and of content."[27] Escarpit thus introduces the social element and, consequently, collective memory into what Greimas calls the "immanent level," the level where conceptual operations take place and are transformed in a way both anthropomorphically and figuratively antecedent to the birth of the linguistic structure of the text.[28] It is here, therefore, that in a certain sense the precedent of communication takes place; in other words, communication is a necessity that is already a part of the deep structure of the artistic process.

If such a rich potential belongs to the competence of the author—along with psychological and sociocultural factors—and consequently such a freedom of choice, then from the moment in which the execution of the text begins, the freedom of the writer is progressively conditioned by the generative structure of the text. As the constructive laws of the work gradually take form, it is the work itself that imposes its will upon the author, a fact to be considered in any theory of the implied author. Wayne Booth, in fact, has suggested the apt definition of "unreliable narrator" for those cases in which a writer, especially a novelist, inserts his own values into the work, values which differ from those of the implied author or constructor of the work and therefore diverge from the "norm of the work," being in contrast with it, and violating the constructive law of the text. The result is, from the point of view of the work's reception and decodification, unreliability.

The problem of the lessening of the author's freedom as the work progresses and dictates its own laws is among the most suggestive of critical-semiological notions. But since it refers mainly to the textual aspect, it falls outside a chapter dedicated to the sender (for this problem see IV.1).

# B.    The Addressee

## 1. INTERNAL AND EXTERNAL ADDRESSEE OF THE WORK

The universe of the addressees of a literary work is the product of ongoing and often uncontrollable relations with the text. Here I shall limit myself to the figure of the addressee of written texts. The oral tradition has special laws of diffusion[1]; and its addressees lack both the visual prop of the written text—which has its own rules—and the reading process itself. (As Segre has recently shown,[2] the reading process introduces among other things a new temporal measure—the time, that is, of reading.) I also exclude the figure of the internal addressee of the book or the *narrataire* as he is called by Gerard Prince in his "Introduction à l'étude du narrataire"[3]: the caliph of the *Thousand and One Nights,* or those who listen for ten days to the novellas of the *Decameron,* as well as the person to whom the author or one of his characters directs remarks or addresses preliminary information. In these cases the relation is internal to the text, it is a part of its structure and is best studied as such. There are historic moments and corresponding literary genres in which the sender of the message invokes the collective attention of his audience with specific formulas (hagiographic texts, *chansons de geste,* for a discussion of which see Zumthor[4]), or else personifies a whole group in one expressly named addressee (for example, the court in courtly poetry). In this regard Auerbach has individuated two modes of address to the reader that are realized in two stylistically different stances: the imperative form and the form that "curries favor" with its covert conative appeal.[5]

This class of addressees, internal to the text, differs in its semiological nature from the class of generic readers; the internal addressee is known on the basis of a precise relation created or hypothesized by the sender. But the generic, impersonal addressee of a text is more problematic; he may be the effective reader, an ideal reader or, finally, a reader hypothesized as virtual or ideal. An awareness of the subtle distinction between the effective, virtual reader on the one hand and the hypothesized reader on the other has considerable importance for a sociology of culture and of literature; applied well, such a distinction would avoid the errors of perspective so frequent in publishing houses and daily newspapers, where choices are often made for a supposed public which does not correspond to the real or virtual public. In other words, there are both a gross presence and a specific audience within the public and it is far easier to gauge the first than the second.

It is perhaps operationally more profitable to distinguish between the relations of the addressee: (a) with the sender, (b) with the work, (c) with the other addressees; in this last case it is the group that creates relations with the work.

## 2. ADDRESSEE-SENDER RELATIONS

The relation that the addressee may establish with the author of the artistic message varies profoundly according to the historical-cultural context. There are eras, like the Middle Ages, in which for ideological motives the concept of paternity and literary property has little importance—hence the large number of anonymous works—and a sphere of indifference is created around the sender. This allows for plagiarism, for additions to the work, for the insertion of portions of other works, without an author's ghost to disturb the peace of the redoer: what really counts is only the great collective process of textual communication. In the fifteenth century, the character of *faber* or *artifex* is attributed to the sender; what is emphasized above all is the technique, the excellence of the craftsmanship and a refined capacity for imitation rather than an absolute individuality or originality, which only begins to attract attention in the sixteenth century. We are, in any case, in the centuries in which writing and reading are the privileges of the intellectual class, so that only from inside that class do we have witnesses: just as Leonardo insists on the value of apprenticeship, so Vasari, in the *Proemio* to the second part of his *Lives of the Painters*, in that part which refers to fifteenth-century artists, declares that all art, literature included, is born "in one through diligence, in another through study, in this one through imitation, in that one from a knowledge of the sciences which come to the aid of these, and in some from all these things together or from the greater part of them."[6] In other words, for Vasari the arts of the fifteenth century outstrip in varying degrees that of the four-teenth century in technical progress, in excellence of crafts-manship. If today, as Gombrich has shown, one can no longer subscribe to Vasari's notion of an organic development of art in time, the fact nevertheless remains—a fact important to my argument—that a knowledge on the part of the public of the quality of *faber* of the artist, changes the sender-addressee rela-tion, eliminating the ritualistic attitude of the medieval public. It was Kris and, following his lead, Gombrich who clarified the new type of reaction, the compensatory nature, in a psycho-analytic sense, of the participation on the part of the addressees in the creative force of the artist and the resulting esthetic satis-faction as a source of regressive pleasure.[7]

With the sixteenth century and Mannerism, the individuality of the sender becomes the subject of speculation, and there is a move toward that process that will explode in Romanticism's emphasis on the individual. In our contemporary age there are at least three forces working to eclipse the figure of the author in favor of the addressee: first, the sociology of literature as practiced by Escarpit, who prefers to emphasize literary facts rather than the text; second, structuralist criticism, which cen-ters on study of the text understood as an object; finally, the critical approach explored by Foucault, with its assertion that an indifference for the author is a fundamental part of the con-temporary concept of *écriture*, which is identical with its own "outstretched exteriority." But Foucault himself justly observes that "to attribute an original statute to writing" is effectively to transfer "into a transcendental anonymity the empirical traits of the author."[8]

Blanchot may denounce—but can hardly mitigate—the situ-ation: "Without knowing it, the reader is involved in a pro-found struggle against the author; despite the intimacy that exists today between the book and the writer, however much the figure, the presence, the biography of the author are directly illustrated in the circumstances of distribution (circumstances which are not fortituous, but perhaps already slightly anachronistic)—despite all this, every reading in which a consideration of the writer seems to have such an important part, is a direct confrontation that annuls him in order to restore the work to itself, to its anonymous presence, to the violent, impersonal affirmation that it exists."[9]

From the point of view of a sociology of literature, the phenomenon of the "practical" rather than the aesthetic use of the work may be of interest: the reader enjoys the work as something belonging to reality and not to artistic creation. For example, he immerses himself in the plot of a novel, he enters it psychologically, feels joy and suffering without an awareness of the work's signedness[10] and therefore without suspecting the activity of its constructor. Such readers remember the narrative events down to the minutest details and ramifications but often do not remember the author's name, an indication of the lack of interest in the addressee for the person who has created and ordered these connections.

The sender-addressee relation is dependent also on the kind of awareness that the author has of his public, a problem that Sartre has faced with acumen. If an author knows, as he did in the Middle Ages, that he has a definite public with a precise ideology, then his function as writer is also definite, he does not suffer the problem of having to discover it, of questioning his own activity: the work already contains in itself an image of the reader for whom it is destined.[11] In modern times, and above all, beginning in the nineteenth century, when the printed book became widely distributed, the author no longer sees his public clearly either because it is potentially so vast or because it cuts across classes and social groups. A sort of detachment results which may allow the author to have an ideology different from that of his readers and to have to decide on the meaning not only of his own work but of literature itself. Sartre cites the example of Richard Wright, who in *Black Boy* knows he is speaking to blacks and whites, knows that "there exists at the heart of his *actual public* a profound break" (Sartre, pp. 125–128). Wright has to face the contradictory needs of his readers, and this confrontation cannot but confer a particular tension to the generative structure of the work.

## 3. ADDRESSEE-WORK RELATIONS

The relation of the addressee to the work is difficult and never linear; it is a mix of psychological, historical, sociocultural, and semiological elements.

Only the semiological level is of central interest to us here; but it may be helpful to outline some of the problems the other levels involve. On the psychological level the reception of the message has, first of all, either the quality of duration or of temporariness. Apart from the banal fact that the text leaves only momentary traces on the reader's psyche, duration is characterized instead either as a unique reading or as the superimposition of different readings on the part of the same person, in effect, as a scuffle between reader and text. This phenomenon—already treated by Blanchot, who considers our every reading unrepeatable[12]—has been acutely examined by Gramigna in *Il testo del racconto*.[13] He describes the discomfort and disorientation of the reader who again takes up a text that he has previously annotated: the prior reader and the actual one no longer communicate, the reappearance of the first is improbable, his underlinings and notations appear undecipherable, tied to a combinatorial mental game that has been lost forever, to a machine that will not start again. Such an event, which has occurred to every attentive reader, must lead to serious reflection on the incomplete autonomy, on the conditioning of our reading, no matter how critical and rigorous it may be. Subtle references to the psychic participation of the reader are also found in Zanzotto (1973), apropos of the sense of the sublime: "One of the characteristics of the sublime according to Dionysius Longinus is that of making us feel things as indeed sublime, as if in some way we ourselves had produced them. Therefore the sublime brings into play the deepest aspects of one's personality, as if we were protagonists engaged in the fable or the drama." In reading, there are gradual repercussions on the individual unconscious and the social unconscious of the addressees, on their memory traces, on what has been called transfigured remembering: a complicated process of action-reaction, the study of which has just begun among specialists.

Within a sociocultural perspective, the problem of the addressee differs according to whether one confronts it from the historical point of view—whether that be diachronic or synchronic—that is, from the point of view of concrete historic addressees differently oriented in conformity with different kinds of culture, or from the theoretical point of view, in which a work, insofar as it is polysemic, can bear the weight of continually accessible meaning and information, giving rise to an unending process of readings by various decoders. The two orders of thinking appear complementary, the first primarily sociocultural, the second, semiological.

Although it is the second that most concerns us here, I should like, by way of example, to make reference to the first. Again, medieval culture beckons us, that Eden of research, by virtue of its highly static symbolism: medieval readers read very differently from us; from the outset they set up a different relationship with the work and with the very function of reading itself, which was of an almost ritualistic nature.[14] Because reading took place in an atemporal, ahistoric, and symbolic atmosphere replete with maxims and formulas that had passed into the collective memory, the reader played the role of participant in a rite, in a ceremony of the diffusion of knowledge accepted by the collective consciousness. Thus, with regard to certain transmissions of medieval texts, we can say that the addressees expected a code more than a message. On the other hand, if the problem is approached from the point of view of social stratification we note that the production of medieval writing (though not, obviously, oral production, which belongs to another discourse) reached only the nobility and the new bourgeoisie. This meant that the addressee differed greatly from what he would be in eras where writing had a greater circulation. Between these two classes it is not the higher, the nobility, but the bourgeoisie (notaries, professors, merchants, et al.) that found itself for historical reasons in the cultural vanguard and therefore better able to decode artistic messages.[15] In this case, since the addressees belonged to limited and well-defined social groups, it is possible to find and study what the sociologists call the "literary personality" of a public.[16] If we turn to an era like ours, the contrast is evident: there is enormous difficulty in finding the "literary personality" of the various strata and social groups that Mury also defines as a "common structure of a plurality of individual I's." The cultural circle is profoundly separated from the popular circle; each has its own literary texts and even, on a pragmatic level, different means and plans for purchase.[17] The distance of the masses from the culture of the elite, the impossibility of their becoming addressees of the literary message (an impossibility investigated by Nicole Robine), is attributable to the lack of a mythology, of a common semiotic-ideolgical system among classes and even social groups. This lack results in the following predicament: "The mass reader rarely is interested in the book that is offered him because he does not have the possibility—as does the reader belonging to the intellectual community—to 're-insert' his product in the network, since he is invited to dispose of something to the construction of which he has not contributed."[18]

Both of these examples—of relation and correspondence (as in medieval literature) and of nonrelation and noncorrespondence (as in mass literature of our day) between the work to be decoded and a social class of addressees—are referable to the synchronic level. Other difficulties arise on the diachronic level because of the intervention of a new type of noncorrespondence: on one side, there is the sociocultural context to which the work is linked; on the other, the very different context to which the addressees are linked. It is no longer a game of two but of four; there is no "situation" in common between sender and addressee but rather one of departure and one of arrival, and the polysemy of the text can generate—instead of ambiguity—confusion. This phenomenon is clearly illustrated by Zumthor, with reference to modern readings of medieval texts: "What, in effect, is a true reading if not a labor in which one finds, simultaneously involved, both the reader and the culture in which he participates? A labor which corresponds to the labor of the one who produced the text—that labor in which the author and his own universe were involved. With regard to a medieval text, the correspondence is no longer spontaneously produced. The very perception of the form becomes equivocal. The metaphors become obscure, the vehicle is separated from the tenor. The reader remains engaged in his own times; the text, through the accumulation of intermediary durations, seems to be outside of time, which is a contradictory situation."[19] From the observations of Zumthor one deduces that in this case the work, on the one hand, speaks less ("the metaphor become obscure") and on the other speaks differently. The first consequence is more grave than the second, indeed from a semiological perspective it is the only grave consequence. If the historical and social being of the addressee leads the reading in a certain direction, that is, if it is proper to speak of a reader-function next to an author-function in the life of a text, then both the sociological and semiological points of view must intersect in the construction of a history of literature that is also a history of readers and a typology of reading, respectively.[20]

## 4. DYNAMIC OF READING

From the perspective of semiology the question of the reader-addressee relationship becomes that of the work's possibility of accumulating information—that is, sign-life—through the various readings it receives in time and space. Borges writes incisively, "The concept of the *definitive text* belongs only to religion or to fatigue." Every text can support an incalculable number of decodifications or destructuralizations; in effect, every text is many texts in that the very nature of its polysemic complexity prevents identically repetitive readings even in the same cultural context. This explains why in certain eras a magical notion of poetry arises and why in our era there has arisen the conception of readings as *variations of a basic invariant,* that is, the text. But while in scientific texts, a hypothesis is considered valid if it is not contradicted by other hypotheses, in the universe of the arts, we are faced with the fact that fundamentally differing interpretations may coexist at the same time—and writers like Eugenio Montale can define such a process as the destiny of poetry in the world.[21]

The degree of polysemy, which may also suggest criteria by which works of art may be hierarchically ordered, cannot be understood by the reader unless he grasps the interaction of the constitutive levels of a work (IV.2). And here one premise is needed: every type of individual communication—and above all, artistic communication—is the result of a process that starts out as a synthesis; it begins as self-communication (the I-I system), and then passes to a communication to be transmitted (the I-he system); and the addressee must of necessity start by a process of analysis, that is, by a partial or total destructuration which allows him to get as close as possible to the synthetic construction of the message, a message which can be seen as a structural tension. Mounin (1969, p. 38) observes: "For the reader also, the genius of others almost always involves long patience." At the end of this complex association the reader can gather the new, highly informative semantic reality of the work; in reaching this reality, the internal relationships of the text, of the words among themselves, count more than the relationship of words and things.[22] In a penetrating image Tasso wrote that the literary work is not an army, not a city, but a universe in which the relations among the elements are dynamic and generate life.

The dynamic of reading corresponds to the dynamic of the

text, and this raises the problem of how the image of the work is constructed and lives in the mind of the addressee. The semiology of literary communication as it refers to the behavior of the addressee inside a system of codes of communication has been treated by Wienold in *Semiotik der Literatur*.[23] But more to the point there is the distinction that Genette[24] makes between two antithetical modes of the reading of a text—as subject or as object. The first mode is bent on identification with the text so that "critical thought *becomes* the thought criticized, and succeeds in refeeling, rethinking, reimagining this thought from within" (Poulet), that is, a kind of intersubjective reading that was defined by Paul Ricoeur as *hermeneutic*. The other mode tends to consider the work as an object, an attitude which brings with it a movement from the external to the internal. In one and the other mode of reading, although they are antithetical at the outset, the text is considered as a closed work (see IV) and the reader tends to perform an operation parallel to that performed by the author. Naturally this process takes place within the limits of the possible, because even the most informed reader cannot but impose his own parameters on the work, cannot look from the outside, as through a glass, at what happens inside. On the limits of the objectivity of reading Starobinski has had many insightful things to say.[25]

There does exist, however, a third approach to the text that contradicts the two preceding ones. This approach, theorized—though in different ways—by both Barthes and Kristeva, tends to deny the intransitivity of the reader and conceives of reading as *re-writing*. According to Barthes, "the place of the literary work (of literature as work) is that of making of the reader no longer a consumer but a producer of the text"; in this function of producer the addressee wants to disseminate the original text, to "disperse it in the field of infinite difference."[26] Kristeva, starting from the concept of the open text or "practice of signification," sees in the addressee the agent who, through semiological destructurations, realizes the expansion of the work's process of semiosis.[27]

The idea of the addressee as producer arises from the conception of the open text; and from the idea of the closed—but not definitively closed—text there arises the idea of the addressee as a collaborator in the polysemic life of the text—a text that never ceases being "made" but also never ceases being linked to its origin. This second perspective appears to me to be the only philologically and historically correct one. It is also the richest one semiologically for two reasons: first, because the very concept of artistic communication requires biunivocality; and second, because it allows for an area of encounter between research that looks for a formal model or the constitutive laws of the work and research that concentrates on the continuing process of decodification.

The three kinds of approaches delineated here refer chiefly to the active participation of the critic in his role as addressee. The median or ordinary reader is especially conditioned by the form of the content of the work or its thematic organization (IV.5). For example, when there is *diegesis*—that is, clear presence of a narrator—the addressee feels himself to be the object of an act of literary communication in which the mimesis can also give him the feeling of witnessing something that is happening. Nevertheless things are really more complex. An author like Brecht said explicitly that he required a double presence: the public that identifies and the public that assumes ideological detachment. In other words, he hoped to divide his theatrical public in two—those who applaud and those who boo—and so to challenge the traditional idea of the text-public relation.

Lotman[28] too studies the average reader. He finds, in the analytic process of decodification, four essential positions of the addressee. Each of these depends on the structure of every work in which there is both a content and the artistic means to handle it and to transfer it onto an artistic level: (1) the reader individuates only the content in its state as matter, raw theme, the prose argument, or poetic paraphrase. The best comment on this improvident reading is offered by Mandelstam: "Poetic analphabetism is confused with the ordinary kind, so that whoever knows how to read is considered poetically literate," with the postscript: "It is certainly easier to electrify all of Russia than to teach all the nonanalphabets to read Pushkin the way it is written";[29] (2) the reader grasps the constructive complexity of the work and the interaction of its levels; (3) the reader willfully extrapolates one level of the work for its exemplary nature (the level of content, or the linguistic or metrical level); (4) the reader who has been esthetically educated comes upon artistic elements extraneous to the genesis of the text, that is, he uses the text for an end different from that for which it was created.

The fourth position reveals an artistic productivity that belongs only to the addressee but which naturally has nothing to do with the concept of addressee-producer of the text that we have found in Barthes; Lotman refers to the artistic decodification of a text that had not been produced for artistic ends. The phenomenon seems to occur with more frequency and intensity when the reader lives in a cultural system different from that in which the work is born; in that case his reading may easily render dominant a textual level which was decidedly not dominant at the moment of composition. Typical in this regard is the artistic fascination exercised on contemporary readers by the didactic or pseudoscientific or purely practical prose of early works in the language because of their linguistic level—lexical or syntactic (phenomena of parataxis, of parahypotaxis, the use of special nominal or paraphrastic constructs, for example) or even phonetic. All these modes were habitual in the language of the time and the reader of that time would have perceived them as normal in his linguistic code.

As is well known, the dynamic of decodification depends, even more than on individual factors, on the cultural and specifically literary system to which the reader belongs. This is why Mukařovský[30] calls the artistic text a "variable measure" and so-called "value," a dynamic reality of the diachronic field. In well-codified cultural systems, like the medieval, the addressee's competence seems greater with regard to texts contemporaneous with him, while in periods of crisis like ours contemporaneity implies less competence. If the work belongs to the past, the reader chooses a method of reading either by following the codifications of his own present system or by following the codifications of the system in which the work was born (for example, compare the reading of Cavalcanti by a poet like Mario Luzi or by a philologist like Domenico De Robertis). If the work—seen diachronically—embodies a variable measure, it is the ensemble of readings that furnishes the sphere or field of significations of the texts. Even the greatest works, those which "speak to everyone" are tied to the inevitability of speaking differently, that is, of being translated by one system of signs into another. In other words, the greatness of a work is directly proportional to the power of its sign-function. In addition, great works adapt themselves, precisely because of their high polysemic level, to readings based on several and diverse models of diverse eras (cf. I.2), and induce the greatest artistic communication: a dialogue of the addressees with the text along the axis of time.

The addressees, therefore, represent a process of personalized, individualized historical knowledge and, with the very crudeness of history itself, they eliminate everything with which they cannot in any way identify or with which they cannot set up a dialogue in the act of reading—with the obvious exception of those cases in which an external imposition, such as the pedagogical, creates an automatic response or a sclerotic reading on the addressee's part. For the same reasons, it is only rarely that texts created for specific addressees contemporary with those texts find an audience beyond their original ambience or survive—their sign-function is limited from the beginning. Think of Italian occasional poetry of the fifteenth and sixteenth centuries: dead, together with the social situations of the "closed" society which nurtured it. The most characteristic example of circular diffusion is that offered by Giovanni Pozzi (1974) in his discussion of the poetic profession at the beginning of the seventeenth century: "This poetry—for the use of producers of poetry and not for a public of simple reviewers—is the correlative of music for performers and not for simple listeners, though the latter kind of music was also prevalent then." Here the consumption takes place on the same level as the production, with an exchange of roles between senders and addressees.

## 5. RELATIONS AMONG THE ADDRESSEES

The scheme proposed in IIb.1 also takes in the relations of addressees among themselves and the social group's relations to the work. In this regard, Sartre wrote: "Among these men who are immersed in the same history and who contribute equally to make it, a historical contact is established through the mediation of the book."[31] It is a contract on the synchronic level but, we should add, also on the diachronic; because through time, the work accumulates information (IIb.4). The critic's activity represents a case in point of the relation between a new reading and all the preceding ones, a case in point of a more or less explicit colloquy with readers dislocated in time.

In a given cultural context the work can engender— arcanely—a relation among its addressees or it can foolhardily submit to the already existing relation. In the first case, the work acts both directly and indirectly, since it reaches even virtual addressees, or nonreaders. A typical example is the work of D'Annunzio which created D'Annunzianism as the estheticizing cultural form of a generation. The indirect action of a work on the linguistic context of a culture is more subtle and enduring when its neologisms and stylemes radiate and become instruments of public communication independent of the reading of the work: a phenomenon very evident in Italy, where literary language, for particular historical reasons, has been the matrix for average and popular language.

However, in the practice of letters the opposite phenomenon also exists: the aggregate of addressees, the public that exists in the background of literature, can produce a system of expectations based on a few constants that influence the creative process. Valéry actually arrives at "an important distinction: that of works *that are as if created by their public* (where they fulfill the expectations and are actually almost determined by the knowledge of this public) and of works that, on the contrary, *tend to create their public.*"[32] Perhaps a tripartite division better reflects reality: the work may favor passively the system of expectations, or favor it actively, or oppose it. In the first case the text fully respects the literary institutions of an era, increases the force of inertia of literature, submits, that is, to the laws of the sociocultural and literary systems that tend to be self-perpetuating. A glaring example is the Italian consumer novel of the Sixties, which achieved the total vagueness of kitsch, a phenomenon that bears witness to how the literary system itself functions; while at the upper level of literature the most sensitive Italian writers intuited the crisis of traditional narrative models, a crisis that was reflected in certain bourgeois values that were inexorably in decline in those years. Other writers, more inclined to favor the expectations of a public interested in products for which it already possessed the reading code, turned out a series of texts in which literary predictability dominated. As Estival already has noted,[33] in these cases the principle of literary causality is overturned and the true starting point is not in the sender but in the addressees; it is the reader who places himself as writer inside the author.

But there are public expectations that have the provocative function of inviting the new. In favoring them the author counterbalances the force of inertia of the system. Auerbach offers illuminating examples of three cultural moments provocative of the new in literary creation: the expectation of the median narrative style in the bourgeois-mercantile class and, correlatively, the *Decameron* of Boccaccio; the expectations of the so-called cultured people and the *Essays* of Montaigne; the *Cour et la Ville* and the stylistic models offered by Boileau.[34] But the most apt and suggestive example is that offered by an author himself, Stendhal, in his *Projet d'article sur "Le Rouge et le Noir."*[35] The writer starts with a description, deliciously humorous, of the two codified types of the consumer novel in the France of his time, the provincial for *femmes de chambre* and the Parisian for *salons*, two real literary genres with specific models of intrigue; nevertheless, he observes, Parisian ladies seem rather saturated with the *amour de coeur* and begin to long for a novelty, *l'amour de tête*, that for which a woman "only loves her lover insofar as she believes herself—each morning—to be on the brink of losing him" and concludes that "this portrait of Parisian love is absolutely new." To describe it thus is to prefigure and realize the expectations of the vast feminine public of Paris; and Stendhal tells us, as he takes on a second role as his own hypothetical reviewer, this happens in *The Red and The Black.*

Finally, there are artistic messages that, in their violation of the collective consciousness, even of the ideological level, break the system of expectations of the addressees. Faced with such "unexpected" messages the readers in the beginning feel their way, disoriented, in the search for that which they cannot find, for a significance that the work does not have; they feel themselves derailed, derouted; the past offers no reading models, and this explains a first phase of uncertainty or outright rejection of works outside the known codifications. It is the difficult destiny that attends works that are rashly innovative or revolutionary (Joyce, Kafka, et al.). But aside from those famous cases, with rare exceptions the strength and the durability of a work depend on its ability to interrupt something (see V.5), an effect noticed more by a public contemporary with the work than by the distant addressee unless the latter reconstructs the historical context. For example, the great stylistic innovation of Galileo has the qualities of a "secondary simplicity" understandable only if considered as the antithesis of the expectations of a public reared on Mannerism.

To conclude, a history of literature that is to include addressees must be, as has been said above, a history of the readers, that is, of the sociocultural context, as well as a typology of reading as a decodification of the literary hypersign. These are two complementary aspects of research; in them the sociology of literature and semiology substitute for their furtive and occasional meetings, a legal union.

# III. The Linguistic Space

## A. *Language and Literary Language*

### 1. QUALITATIVE DIFFERENCE

At the center of linguistic creation stands the language of the artist. His text actualizes the greatest number of the potentialities of language; from the syntagmatic, transsentential links of the text, a secondary semantic of a higher level is produced; the language of the artist has the status of a supersign-function[1] (see IIIb.3). In the language of the literary text there flow together—with varying force, ascertainable case by case—the language of communication and literary language. Such intermingling suggests that it does not seem profitable to contrast the language of the text with language itself—as is often done in the field of linguistics—without taking into account the active mediation of literary language, that pawnshop from which every writer has drawn, leaving something as a pledge. One can only agree with Van Dijk: "All approaches to a definition of literature that try to reduce it to a specific 'use' of standard language or to a specific 'function' of language (Jakobson, 1960) thus overlook the important fact that it is a *specific language-system, within a language L but different from $L_N$, describable by an autonomous but non-independent grammar.*"[2] Such a recognition has theoretical implications, already recognized by Barthes when he saw the need for an extension of the rules of literary language, a starting point for a "science of discourse": "The author, the work, are not the beginning of an analysis

50

whose horizon is language; there cannot be a science of Dante, of Shakespeare or of Racine, but only a science of discourse. This science will have two large areas, according to the signs of which it treats: the first will include the lower signs of the sentence, of ancient figures, the phenomena of connotation, 'semantic anomalies,' etc., in brief all the traits of literary language in its ensemble; the second will include the higher signs of the sentence, the parts of discourse where one can *intuit* a structure of the *récit*, of the poetic message, of the discursive text, etc."[3]

Granger, in his turn, insists on the necessity of distinguishing *a priori* codes that belong in part to the language of communication and in part to the language of literature ("The notion of literary genre, though generally more vague than that of grammar, must be considered as being part, as long as it is efficacious, of *a priori* codes") from *a posteriori* codes that are produced with the message.[4]

The most advanced theory we have today on literary language as a formal system, a system present unconsciously also in the addressee of any text (who can distinguish, though in varying degrees, between literary and nonliterary texts) is that of Van Dijk, who concerns himself with the problem of the specific in literary language. In his schema, $G_N$ indicates the general textual grammar and $G_L$ that of the literary text. He arrives at the formulation $G_L - G_N = C$, where C is the sum of the complementary rules proper to the literary system. In its turn C includes $C_M$ = the series of rules that modify general grammar, and $C_S$ = a series of specific rules that operate on specific categories—alliteration, rhyme, specific lexicon, etc. Stated schematically, C represents the sum of rules of transformation and formation proper to literary language. The result is that $G_L$ has a capacity and generative force greatly superior to $G_N$. This means that there is a qualitative difference in the literary language with respect to language itself: "The difference thus also lies at the qualitative level: $G_L$ does not merely specify a more extensive language, it also provides more adequate structural descriptions."[5] This is the reason why, as was stated above, the mere application of linguistic grids in the examination of literary language misses its specific properties and sign-functions; in fact, if it is true that alliteration, rhythmic solutions, tropes, parallelisms, etc., appear also in everyday language at the spoken level, what is lacking in these cases is the constructive, interrelated function that is typical of literary language. I should add in this regard that the interrelation of textual levels in the literary work or even in the programs and codifications of traditional literary genres also works as a de-familiarizing artifice for linguistic statements that are well formed from the point of view of $G_N$ (see IIIb.4).

The competence of the already mentioned complementary rules (C) belongs to the senders or producers of the artistic messages; again it is Van Dijk who uses the terminology *competence-system* or *performance-system* as against the individual *performance*—in which the author produces individual deviations and transformations; the latter, as we well know, can result from conscious or unconscious situations and requires an approach that leads us inside the single textual unit, that is, a more specific inquiry by the critic. We can add that the label *performance-system* is clearly referable to literary theories of style. We will be more cautious than Van Dijk regarding the "secondary competence" of the addressees, because they may miss, especially in dealing with a noncontemporary work, the implications of codes distant in time and created in a different semiological cultural system (see IIb.3).

## 2. LANGUAGE FROM THE POINT OF VIEW OF THE POETS

If we pass from the universe of the theorists to that of the poets and of their reflections on the making of poetry, here too we find that reality is both enriched and split up. In commenting on the recent volume *Rimario* by Antonio Porta, Andrea Zanzotto demonstrates that Porta's poetry is not a combinatorial game of rhyme fixed on the page, but a "recognition, arrived at through soundings that could be continued to infinity, of the *living* consistency of linguistic structure, felt as an immense 'aura of resonance' in which the semantic and sign circuits condition each other, augment each other and help to 'discover' each other. But more: in line with what present research is revealing, Porta in his work seems to hypothesize the existence of a personal 'rhyming-dictionary' for everyone—a dictionary that is connected to the history of his individuation, almost as if the formation of linguistic competence coincided with the structuration of the 'I.'"[6] This is equivalent to saying that the complex of language, common and literary, is felt by the artist as something that has in itself an extraordinary potential; it is a treasure of primordial suggestions, of coagulations, of phonic-rhythmic facts that attract each other. It is a mysteriously oriented living material in whose interstices the artist moves, and he moves according to an individual law that is nothing other than one of the possible directions in which the potentials of language can be realized.

Besides Porta's *Rimario,* Zanzotto in the same article offers the example of the nonsense jingles of Meneghello in *Pomo Pero:* "The original (Ur) tablets of the world that is the village of Malo are given in texts formed by dialect words (in part fallen into disuse) that are mutually attracted and drawn together through means that seem only homophonic and homorhythmic. These dialect words, however, finally define themselves with dense and even coactive completeness." The particular sensation that an addressee or reader experiences when confronted by texts such as Porta's *Rimario* and Meneghello's jingles is that of feeling himself an active part and not only an addressee; he is implicated in a poetic operation in which he can collaborate, in a dissemination of signifiers and meanings that he can extend and amplify, under the direction of his own language, whose potentialities he is led to discover.

Seen thus, it is less the divergences of language and literary language, and more their links that are emphasized; literary language does not appear in its role as a codifying system but as a catalyst for the potential that resides in language itself.

## 3. LITERARY COMMUNICATION AND LANGUAGE

I pass from general considerations to those of a historic and diachronically pragmatic nature. In Italy—for instance—common language, that is, the language of real life, involved in the praxis of communication, is of recent origin, whereas literary language, which has exceptional longevity, has been organized through the centuries into a system of cultural communication. This system is used not only by writers, and it is endowed with such capacity for endurance that it can gradually transmit to the future the models of the past. A special example is the hardy resistance, through time and social change, of the ideal (or convention) of Tuscan literary language in a literature like the Italian with its innumerable regional centers. On this level the deviation of the single artistic message cannot be measured without taking into account a background of centuries of strong linguistic-literary dogma. In the sixteenth century the formal codification of a Tuscan or Florentine type was imposed as a norm on non-Tuscan authors; when Machiavelli in his *Discorso o dialogo intorno alla nostra lingua* describes the situation of "foreign" Italians for whom "it is useful to come to Tuscany; or if indeed they make use of their [native] words, they smooth and enlarge those words in the Tuscan manner, since otherwise neither they nor others would approve of them," he demonstrates fully the phenomenon of the canonization of one level, the linguistic, among the many literary conventions. The phrase "neither they nor others would approve of them" is the precise evidence of a situation in which both the producers of the message and the addressees have a common code, which in this case even has a normative character, that justifies approval or disapproval. Further on Machiavelli introduces Ariosto as an example of the impossibility of writing good plays except in Tuscan and he adds: "It therefore follows that he who is not Tuscan will never do this well, because if he wants to express the sayings of his own homeland he will create a patchwork, a composition half Tuscan and half foreign. . . . But if he doesn't want to do this, not knowing the Tuscan [expressions], he will produce a work that is wanting and that will not achieve perfection"—the case of Ariosto. And so we watch the phenomenon of a formal convention leading to linguistic taboos (against the use of regional forms), and of a writer as great as Ariosto so conditioned by such taboos on one of the levels in which his work as dramatist was organized. In Italy the confraternity of Tuscan vowels and consonants advanced in stately procession, while to the side regional forms skittered and skipped or tramped.

Within the linguistic and stylistic level itself the degree of stability of the force of inertia of the literary system varies from convention to convention: the codification of poetic language, we know, has been more tenacious and rigorous than that of prose, and the genre of lyric poetry more so than any other. It is of interest that the first use in Italy of the term "code" to indicate a closed and partially normative tradition of poetic language was not by a semiologist but by a philological expert who used it in describing the language of Sicilian poetry. Santorre Debenedetti, in his essay on Stefano Protonotaro,[7] proposed Sicilian poetry as the first example of the crystallization of Italian literary language: to the fixed thematic level, which allows us today to draw up repertories of topoi, motifs, and symbolic functions, there corresponds on the formal level a precise network of linguistic codifications (phonic level, phonic-rhythmic, syntactic, metric, lexical), a network which has traversed the centuries with uniform acceptance.

Only in the nineteenth century did the need emerge to transfer literary language to a level of communication available to society at large and not just to an elite public. Contemporary poetry and prose have taken a further step in that direction, but at the same time the Italian language as a whole has also advanced in the direction of a general means of social communication; today some writers have shown a rather radical hostility to traditional literary language, which they see as a language that, forever pregnant with history, lives on a stage. For them the literary codes are expressions of specific social classes, reductive in their organizing function and—at least in part—masking and harboring an ideology. This attitude accelerates various processes and alters the relations between the writer and language: on the one hand there is the recourse to daily spoken language, on the other to the shrill universe of specialized jargons[8] and of the mass media.

In the first case, the notion of daily language must be well specified every time it enters into written language and is incarnated in a style.[9] Blanchot had already observed how quotidian language "communicating to us the illusion of the immediate while it gives us only the habitual, has the power to make us believe that the immediate is familiar."[10] To this property of everyday language must be added the aggravating factor of the current explosion of standards, of linguistic consumerism, against which Lefebvre often and passionately—and at some length—protests: in our consumer society, language "becomes a fetish; instead of referring to something—content, praxis, sense data—discourse becomes referential for groups that have nothing more in common than gossip because nothing relates them to productive or creative activity."[11] Ordinary language can run the risk of having not an immediate reality behind it but the false referents of technological reality. Thus one arrives at the paradox that, in an era of frenzied theorizing about communication, it is actually authentic communication among people, the natural pact of communication, that is weakening to the point of becoming silenced by "standard" communication.

The poet knows that today in the territory of ordinary language there are no goat paths—only paved roads. Therefore his relation to language cannot be immediate but requires operations that take place in two chief directions. In one direction he can attempt to act against the forgetfulness that overtakes the speakers of a language; he can recuperate the potential that resides in the living material of language, the changing dispositions (already referred to in section 2), and in this way actuate the great *linguistic and ideological function of poetic communication.* [12] In the other direction he can produce, with appropriate calculation, a demystification or linguistic defamiliarization of the formal codifications of the language. This second attitude also involves the artist's recourse to the false delectations of specialized jargons, to the blather of the mass media, a universe that has recaptured with various formal tricks—note the coincidence—precisely those elements of the literary tradition of the past of which the artist has found himself most suspicious. Wandruszka—using a very unlikely coinage—has called these elements *poetolects,* vying with the *technolects* and *sociolects.* [13] Such maneuvers on the part of the artist are certainly not really new: even Mallarmé said that he served to the bourgeoisie the words they read every day in the papers, but served them in a "derouting combination" [*combinaison déroutante*]. Such derouting results in a positive disturbance in the linguistic consciousness of the addressee. Thus Zanzotto (1973), commenting on his own poem *Gli sguardi i fatti e senhal,* says: "If in this poem there has been a reliving and 'rekneading' of numerous myths that have represented real constants of the human collective psyche, there are also, in the foreground, the typical circumstances of the frightening and terrible consumption of words and images that occurs today." So that, apropos the "reams of useless chatter" served up by cinema and television, Zanzotto conjures the planet surrounded by "a sphere of celluloid and tape excrement with visions and blather embalmed inside." Analogously, in the poetry of Antonio Porta language is sometimes registered as words without connotations or denotative meaning—only pure and superfluous noise.

When profound transformations in the ideology and social context react so radically on the expressive level—in both literary language and language—this is an indication that the very concept of literature is in crisis, which in fact has happened (see I.4, V.3).

## 4. CODES AND REGISTERS OR ''MODES OF WRITING''

In a general way one can think of the writer's linguistic activity as a daring game of oscillation between his own individual language or idiolect and literary language, which he absorbs from the context of his age and from the reading of texts of the past. It will be useful now to consider further this latter reading, which has had such an astonishing influence in Italy, for the historical reasons referred to above. Obviously, I do not want to drown in the great sea of bibliography devoted to the literary language (that bibliography was particularly enriched during the phase of stylistic criticism; it will be found treated epoch by epoch in any textbook). I want rather to indicate the essential problems involved in a semiological interpretation of literary communication.

Ordinary language and literary language represent two different inscriptions of the historical situation in the language, and therefore two modalities for realizing linguistic signs; it is for the author to exercise his freedom of choice. In neglecting the dialectical relation of the author's acceptance of, allusion to, contrast with, or refusal of literary language, one runs the risk of losing part of the new meaning of the text. For this dialectic is a dimension not only of the linguistic, but of the critical-semiological order; the fact that some authors follow the official track while others travel more freely has a particular sign-function.

In literary language the possibilities of signification and communication are realized differently than they are in language, not only for the general and structural reasons outlined above (section 1) but because literary language is a connotative system that accumulates diachronically. The word or syntagm or styleme is not only connotative in itself; it also has an extra semantic element, a surplus of significations which derives from the earlier artistic contexts in which it has occurred; think of the evocative weight that adheres to the adjective *vago* [Not only does it mean "vague," but its "indefiniteness" passes into "appealing in a sweet, indefinite way" or "intimately pleasing, with a mixture of grace and tenderness"—with many other resonances.—A.M.] through the long Italian poetic tradition, or to the adjective *ermo* [solitary] after its use by Leopardi. One conspicuous form of diachronic accumulation is the codifications of literary language. Allowing for the errors inherent in all schemes, we may distinguish the following elements within literary language:

(1) Stylistic codes in well-delimited environments, codes that belong to the various literary genres and to various eras and that represent the spatial-temporal vitality of several formal constants structured in relation to specific thematic material (see chap. V). This fixed and bidirectional relation from themes to forms and forms to themes allows us to use the term "code."

(2) Formal consolidated subsystems or registers or modes of writing or styles whose birth, life, and death are conditioned by the dialectic of sociocultural phenomena. As Auerbach has shown so well in *Mimesis*, there exists, in consequence, the transmigration of a series of linguistic facts from one stylistic level to another with the passage of time. For example, in ancient literatures and language, parataxis belongs to the humble style and has a character more comic-realistic than sublime, whereas in the *Chanson de Roland*, as in the autonomous tradition of the Bible, paratactic members with the force of independent linguistic blocks are the syntactic structure of a high style, the sublime.[14] However, if styles are studied on a synchronic level, as in Barthes' investigations of writing, then they manifest a closed quality, which has led Barthes to say: "One will find therefore in every writing the ambiguity of an object that is both language and coercion; at the bottom of writing there is a 'circumstance' extraneous to language, something like the look of an intention that is no longer that of language."[15]

Styles or registers or types of writing have always responded to the demands of an author, offering something both more organized and more schematic than the texts on which he has been formed—something similar to a formal model. These types of writing account for the presence of recognizable traits in the works of writers who conform to them. That is, the elements that issue from a type of writing or register (be they phonetic, morphosyntactic, or lexical) carry with them, along with the semantic content, "supplementary information about the register."[16] Phonetically, an example would be the persistence down to the end of the ninteenth century in Italian lyric poetry of the nondiphthong forms *foco, loco,* etc., while prose contains the diphthong forms—*fuoco, luogo*—that also belong to many regional dialects. Still, a conscious stylistic effect can be achieved by extra-register means: these are what Riffaterre calls *nonce-standards* or the use of conventional structures with a defamiliarizing effect, for example, aulic forms of the high style inserted in parodistic texts.

(3) Rhetoric, that great code of connotation, or product of hypercodification,[17] the rules and formal practices of which have spanned the centuries because of its capacity to accommodate diverse contents. Bice Garavelli Mortara observes: "As distinct from grammar (*ars bene loquendi*), which fixed the norms of correct speech on the basis of 'good authors' but did not furnish any criterion for the study of texts, limiting its analysis to words and sentences—rhetoric, didactically occupied with style, arrived at dismantling and defining the mechanisms of discourse and of tracing global plans for the structuring of content."[18] So that rhetoric is a foundation not only of the theory of styles but even of the concrete existence of certain types of writing.

However, today something new has occurred. In our contemporary cultural context the presence and function of rhetoric are strong, even stubborn, but with characteristics different from those of the past. There has been much renewal in the theoretical field: that the *nouvelle rhétorique* descends from classic rhetoric but differs from it in its logical, philosophical, and sociological attitudes and in its basic qualities has again been made clear in recent studies by Vasoli on the *Traité de l'argumentation* of Perelman and Olbrechts-Tyteca (see the bibliography in note 17). Also new is the contact between research in this field and general theories of textual grammar (cf. the chapter, "Semantic Operations. Processes of Metaphorization" in Van Dijk, 1972), and between theoretical research and its application in semiology to literary facts and their constitutive levels. What has emerged is a program for a rationalized typology of rhetorical figures (the already cited *Rhétorique générale* of the Liège group). Naturally things are more complex—not least because every rhetorical figure, as we know, contains its own small "Homeric" problem, still under discussion.

We now have to ask whether one can find in current linguistic practice (in language and literary language) something that corresponds to this renewal of interest in rhetoric on the theoretical and critical level. The answer differs according to whether we fix our inquiry on literary production or on production (written or oral) in the special sectors of language. Contemporary literature does not allow us a single answer: recently Baehr in an article "Retorica rediviva?" (see note 17) concludes a brief discussion of the differences between the use of rhetorical figures in the French *nouveau roman* and in Italian narrative and gives the edge to the latter. In general one can say that the relations between living writers and traditional rhetorical models are not straightforward; as against the ruptures and rejections on the part of some (see I.4, IIIa.6), there are the noisy revivals of outright Manneristic structures on the part of others (see V.6). Instead, rhetorical models have extended their influence in a sometimes overpowering way into various areas of social communication to the point where the study of some specialized languages—of politics, advertising, sports, etc.— turns into research on the application of these models.

The different results on the literary and pragmatic levels point up the fundamental connections between the rhetorical phenomenon and the social situation. The possibility that rhetorical rules set in motion the connotative function of language, that is, all the hidden forms of persuasion, explains the emergence of rhetoric today in pragmatic areas; to place rhetorical fences around the enunciation of things helps to hide them.[19] Thus we find an analogy in rhetoric for what is happening to literary genres (see I.4, V.3): a functional crisis on the upper artistic level and an increase in mass communication in the form of empty and lively packaging. It would perhaps be simplistic to create structural homologies—as Goldmann has done—between social history and changes in the use of rhetoric, even if, as Barthes noted as long ago as 1967, history subtly modifies the rhythm of formal transformations and, we should add, the place and social level of their occurrence.[20] Briefly then, on the consumer level we see the perpetuation of traditional models with a showy use of figures of words and thought, while in literary language it is the problematic use of the traditional and its transformations that interest us.

To the rhetorical structure of literary language, understood as a diachronic development, we owe the fact that a certain number of figures, syntagms, and stylemes, true rhetorical markers, have assumed such an autonomous sign-force as to be able to move in differing times and places independently of the registers of stylistic code or simple text in which they originated. Jean Cohen gives examples of habitual figures (*figures d'usage*), "where form and substance, relations and ends are discounted. Thus in the expression *flamme si noir* (Racine) we have an apparently bold formula that in reality contains no trace of invention. *Flamme* for *amour*, *noir* for *coupable* are a normal usage in that age: their intelligibility for a cultured public is immediate."[21] However, while for Cohen the expression "*figures d'usage*" is a contradiction in terms in that "the usual is the negation of the deviant," for Genette there is validity in the rhetorical distinction between "*figures d'usage*" and "figures of invention" in that the deviation is defined by its opposition to a literal meaning, not by its opposition to use,[22] and the entire history of rhetoric and literary language confirms him. The traditional metaphors, now deprived of the original force that had been produced by the metaphorizing process within a context, constitute what Van Dijk defines—as had Chafe and Des Tombes—as a "literary lexicon" comparable to an "idiomatic or 'performance' lexicon."[23] We still lack a history of the Italian literary language which relates a typology of styles to the shifting rhetorical microstructures and gives indices of their frequency.

The ensemble of rhetorical markers as well as traditional rhetorical material and codified stylistic elements is very important for literary communication because it eases the encounter of the text and the addressee; it offers the presence of the already known alongside the newness of the message and favors communication on its first level.

## 5. SYNCHRONIC AND DIACHRONIC ANALYSES OF LITERARY LANGUAGE

One of the postulates of Doležel in "Zur statistische Theorie der Dichtersprache" is that the linguistic structure of a work requires an examination of literary language on both the synchronic and diachronic levels, because the poetic language of a text produces deformations not only of the language contemporaneous with it but also of the tradition of the literary language that precedes it: "The explication of the linguistic structure of a literary work, a literary school, or a literary period can only be carried out by linking synchronic analysis to historical (diachronic) analysis."[24] Synchronic and diachronic aspects are not only needed for textual analysis; they are indispensable for discovering the principles of the literary system. The formal constants of that system—as already perceived by the Russian Formalists—change function in the course of time and codifications can be so transformed in time as to be eventually lost, save for possible later recovery. The stronger and more pervasive the formal code in the system—as the rhetorical code, for example—the longer it is destined to endure, while codifications linked to a single literary genre—for example, bucolic poetry—are subject to a relatively brief life. This problem will be discussed again in Chapter V in relation to literary genres, so that here I shall give only one brief example, taken from a synchronic section of literary language, fifteenth-century Italian. Latin, always napping in the wings in Italian, awakens completely in this age, so that one of the determining innovations consists in the new literary use within the vernacular of a whole series of Latinisms—phonetic, morphological, syntactic, lexical—all rising and growing under the influence of the strongest and most fecund cultural movement of the century, Humanism.

Two fundamental facts then emerge: (1) the entrance of the new material and of the new linguistic functions changes the organization of relations of the elements that had previously constituted the literary language. A coaxial change in the internal relations of the system also takes place (for example, many fourteenth-century forms are eclipsed); (2) both the limited stylistic codes (literary genres) and the great consolidated formal subsystems or styles or registers (for the distinction, see above, section 4) avail themselves of Latin for their own purposes, thus conferring on these systems a specific sign-function. For example, in the bucolic genre the massive introduction of Latinisms creates a series of *sdrucciole* rhymes (with stress on the antepenultimate) that crop up with the same words from text to text (*angere, baculo, vetera,* etc.). This organically transforms the rhythmic-metric level by means of the poets' compositional strategy, which is also phonic-rhythmic. In addition, these Latin words become, because they play against the bucolic lexicon, carriers of a symbolic meaning (shepherd = Humanist) and acquire a new level of signedness.[25] Eclogues can in this way become the bearers of a symbolic discourse of a political nature, hence of a semantics of many steps, of many isomorphic levels (see IV.4).

But in the Petrarchism of the fifteenth century, the grafting of Latinisms on to the model of a well-codified poetic language serves to create a vital eclecticism in which Petrarch is no longer the only component of the movement that bears his name. Latinisms are case by case symptoms or signals of a new poetic.[26]

It is not easy to distinguish in these two examples how much depends on individual poets and how much on the sphere of extratextual reference, that is, on literary language with its socioideological motivations. It is therefore indispensable when studying the single text, to keep an eye on what can be called the *"figura oppositiva,"* the relation, that is, between an enunciation present in the text and other possible enunciations offered by the literary tradition—the sum of presences and absences, that is to say, of choices. What counts most in all this is the diverse function of the constant Latinism in several kinds of formal codifications on the synchronic level.

When we turn to the diachronic level, the examples of constant form with a changing function multiply; the invariant signifies the lower limit of pertinence of the collective work of writers that will change the function. For example, there is the expressionistic thread where the invariant is the composite language (a meeting of Latinisms, archaisms, dialects, aulic and popular forms and techniques) that is exploited historically in the vital course of the expressionistic current and adjusted to different sociocultural contexts. Gadda speaks incisively of developments that exceed the confines of personality and helps us to conceive of a history of literature in a collective sense.[27] And several studies of expressionism (Contini, Segre, et al.) have shown in detail how from the thirteenth (the *Contrasto* of Cielo d'Alcamo) to the sixteenth century (Folengo, Ruzante) to the nineteenth century (the Scapigliati) to today (Gadda and the Gaddians), writers on the one hand have shifted the mutual relations of the registers—that is, have made innovations in their procedures—and on the other hand have conferred on this linguistic composite a different function in the text, and therefore in the ideological message offered to the addressees. In Folengo, for example, what strikes us is the enrichment on the constructive plane of the invariant (= composite language). One thinks of the combinatorial game of the dialectal elements, made up of the koine of the southeast Po Valley or of specific dialects (Mantuan, Brescian, Bergamasque, etc.) all kneaded together with the normal literary language of the sixteenth century and a highly mobile Latin.[28] Or, think again of the mainly ideological function of the ninteenth-century expressionism of Carlo Porta.[29] The latest and most recent example is to be found in *Horcynus Orca* by Stefano D'Arrigo,[30] an epic poem in prose, more a modern *cantare* than a novel, in which the combinations of the formal elements of the expressionistic line (aulic language, Latinisms, various Sicilian dialects of the Straits of Messina area) serve the function of giving a linguistic body to the mythic-historic stratification (pagan-Christian) of the marine culture of Sicily, the island scene of the vast epic. We are at a cosmic distance here from the expressionism of the *Contrasto* of Cielo d'Alcamo.

## 6. THE LINGUISTIC INNOVATION OF THE WRITER

To shift perspective, we can pose the problem of the influence of the writer's linguistic innovations on the two systems of language and literary language. The writer's relation to language is less directly accessible because the codified solidity of the system is such that the individual innovation works very slowly and through various mediations, except perhaps in exceptional periods like the nineteenth century in regard to Manzoni's linguistic solution. But in literary language the innovative yeast can work swiftly: in the history of literary language even the drastic breakthrough achieved by a writer or an avant-garde movement may pass quickly and spawn its imitators, and so the "breakaway genre" is born. We shall postpone to Chapter V a more detailed discussion of the crises in the codes caused by the authentic writer, and only anticipate the problem here by offering two extreme examples of the relation between the artist's language and literary language.

Dante lived in an era of strong literary codification and robust theorizing about style, and he accepted their importance on the theoretical level. In fact the *De vulgari eloquentia* demonstrates this concern, and it is restated in the letter to Cangrande della Scala, written after the *Commedia*. But in the *Commedia* itself, Dante violates the laws of a closed style and makes profound innovations which are at war with theoretical limitations and the separation of styles. Auerbach notes how Benvenuto da Imola had already understood the problem when he explained that the three styles—the illustrious-tragic, the middle polemical-satiric, and the humble-comic—were all present in the *Commedia*.[31] Now Dante is a writer who, as Petrocchi says, always "knows what he thinks and what he does,"[32] and therefore offers the highest testimony of the way in which a great writer cannot but disturb the peace of the literary waters, of those public norms of writing that he believed he had accepted. The formal laws of the work impose themselves on the stylistic canons with a differentiating force, and Dante is immersed in innovation as in his own element. In the Thirties Mandelstam described this phenomenon brilliantly in his *Discourse on Dante:* "Long before Bach, before the building of monumental organs, when there were only modest prototypes, embryos for the future, when the lyre accompanied by the human voice was still the chief instrument, Dante knew how to construct in verbal space a potent and immeasurable organ on which he was already able to satisfy his whims, using all the possible registers, blowing on the bellows, making all the reeds shout and whisper."[33]

The phenomenon of the break with stylistic conventions on the part of a great writer has already been studied on the semiological level by Lotman (1970); but different and, at this point in our discussion, relevant to the case of Dante is the double nature of Dante's programmatic range, theoretical on one side and poetic-creative on the other; at the moment when the theorist inserts himself into the tradition, the poet surges beyond it. If one accepts the distinction Van Dijk makes between the formal macrostructures of a text on its deep level (in the sense that linguistics uses "deep") and the microstructures of the surface, then perhaps Dante's fidelity to the rules of style takes place on the first level; whereas the polyphony, to use Mandelstam's musical image, takes place on the second level, conditioned by contextual reasons. In the work of Dante, a coherent macrostructure is manifested through local discontinuous structures that have great innovative power in relation both to the text and to the tradition of literary language.

The second example—a *parva componere magnis* with respect to the first—offers an inverted relation between theoretical reflection and creation; and only because of this inversion can it be compared. It has to do, that is, with a strong theoretical awareness of the need to break with the literary tradition and, for that very reason, with the lack of a corresponding richness in the results of experimentation. It is the case of the Italian neoavant-garde of the Sixties with its fruitful devastation of the linguistic-literary tradition, its calling into question the system of codification, its special contest (*tenzone*) with all linguistic material, literary or not, in which it saw only the prolongation of the norms of the past. Its justifications have been clearly recapitulated after the fact by Guglielmi: "The logical ruptures, the syntactic fragmentations show that we are in the presence of a symbolic regression from a logical-syntactic order, in which the practical and dialectical word is crystallized and transformed into 'truth' or into ideological sublimation—to a semantic order, that is, to those informal meanings, in part unconscious, that obey a logic very different from that of communication, a logic that ideological sublimations are no longer enough to contain and subordinate. The avant-garde descends the steps of the alienation of language and poses the problem of changing the world (even *changer la vie*)."[34] For such reasons the writers of the neoavant-garde are all less able to construct than destruct; they use the old codes in an abnormal way rather than creating new ones; they de-mystify, challenge, are evasive. The coincidence between lucid theory and poetic praxis is here at the base of the impossibility of creation. The memorable protagonists in these texts are precisely literary language and language themselves, both subjected to a process of confrontation, to a categorical test of their reality.[35]

# B. The Distinctiveness of Poetic Language

## 1. POETRY AND PROSE

In practice it is not possible to set a limit, a partition, between texts that are poetic and those that are not, so minimal are the gradations from the nonpoetic to the poetic, so hard is it to determine where language begins to be poetic—even though one knows that theoretically a distinctive criterion for poetry does exist. Therefore it is more fruitful to investigate poeticality by examining the last links in a hypothetical chain of texts with an arrow directed toward poetry; and among these texts I shall opt for the poetic text in verse, although there is no theoretical reason for excluding prose poems and poetic prose. These latter categories, however, do not appear in Jean Cohen's classification,[1] where the "poem in prose" is made to coincide with the "semantic poem," that is, a text that does not utilize the phonic-tonal aspect of language, the aspect that determines the poetic message. Thus Cohen remains curiously anchored to the old, simplified distinction between verse texts and non-verse texts. Instead one must take into account that apparent prose, called poetic or art prose, whose characteristic is the parity of rights, the absolute equality given to sound and sense, to the signified and the signifier—an equality that does not belong to the typology of prose as such. Here is Zamjatin: "In what does the difference between prose and poetry consist?

Does it really exist? The poets, the versifiers still claim the privilege of constituting a special artistic church. But for me it is obvious: between poetry and art prose there is no difference. They belong together. . . . To be an authentic master in art prose is as difficult as completing an interplanetary voyage."[2] An excellent example might be the *Arcadia* of Jacobo Sannazaro, whose prose is a striking example of a structurally organized phonic-rhythmic measure, interacting with the semantic level to the point of semanticizing the elements of timbre and rhythm as in any respectable poetic text. The prose of *Arcadia* is actually more poetic than the eclogues it serves to frame. Another great archetype of lyric prose is Dante's *Vita Nuova*.[3]

It is, in any case, undeniable, and can be confirmed by everyone's mnemonic inventory, that the prose-poetry relation is established by very different criteria from one literature to another and from one era to another, as Lotman had already noted.[4]

## 2. THE POETIC PRE-TEXT AND THE DOUBLE ''*ENTRÉE EN JEU*''

Of what are we speaking when we speak of poetic language? The fundamental problem, one which has been posed from the distant reflections of ancient Indian theoreticians right up to the present, has a double aspect: (1) What are the specific qualities of poetic language? and (2) Is there a qualitative difference between the respective relations of poetry and "ordinary" writing to language, despite their use of the same material? The second question belongs to the general problem of the differentia of literary language in itself (for a discussion of which see IIIa.1).

The first question obviously is not merely linguistic, in that it embraces the question of poetic competence and the developmental process of creative energy; that is, it concerns something that looms over the execution of the text but belongs to the pre-text or to the pre-textual generative phase. Pre-text here certainly does not mean *hors-text* as in Duchet (1971, p. 8). Creative energy consists of input into the pre-text. In a beautifully grammatical image, Mandelstam sees as improper every notion of the work of art as a static object, ready-made, having "the Buddhist and upper-school quiet of the nominative case."[5] To understand more, he adds, it is necessary to take into account the dynamics of creation. It is useful, therefore, to begin with those dynamics in order to understand how poetic language resists and violates ordinary language as a means of communication and as a code.

The Indian theoreticians had already posed the problem; and their solution, although unacceptable in our cultural context, is highly significant and stimulating. As Pierre Sylvain Filliozat has shown (1972), for these theoreticians, poetic language is sound that produces knowledge. Up to here, the formula is acceptable and even, in a certain sense, very modern. The text is a chain of phonic-rhythmic resonances, comparable for the Indians to the prolonged resonances of a bell. Why does this chain of resonances produce a knowledge that goes deeper than the normal knowledge of reality? Because, according to these Indian theoreticians, there lives again in the poetic word an ancient sign, deposited in the depths of the psyche; and this word reveals anterior traces, memories of referents of the past encountered by man in prior incarnations. Now, if we violate this Indian meditation by freeing it from the philosophic-religious embrace of the theory of reincarnation, we are left with several ideas whose significance has spanned the centuries: (a) poetry is sound that offers us knowledge; (b) the poetic word has a density of signification or an ingrained polysemy which belongs to it only in the poetic context; (c) this density is connected to pre-textual processes.[6]

Moving to our times and sampling some remarks of poets regarding the pre-text phase, what strikes us is the repetition of many similar statements about such dissimilar products. Valéry: "And sometimes it is a will to expression that starts the game, a need to translate what one feels; but sometimes, it is quite the opposite, an element of form, an expressive outline that searches for its cause, that searches out a sense in the space of my soul. . . . Observe well this possible duality in the *entrée en jeu:* sometimes something wishes to be expressed, sometimes some means of expression wants something to serve."[7] Both aspects of the process bear reflection. Elsewhere, Valéry defines this potential duality of the *entrée en jeu* through the expressions *combinaison des choses* (combination of things) and *combinaison des mots* (combination of words) with an important postscript or with supplemental information regarding the first phrase (I, p. 1454): the poet "sees figures in a particular order where another sees only what interests a chance observer." This other way of seeing the real, which involves the capacity to move around and rearrange its elements, is described by Pasternak: "Everything happens as if reality were to emerge through a new category; this category seems to us to be its own state, not ours . . . we try to give it a name. Thus art is born."[8]

The genesis of this new "category," which seems to be the real's "own state" but is instead produced by the relation between the real and the "state" of the subject, has also been treated by René Char: "Imagination consists in expelling from reality many incomplete persons and, through the action of the magical and subversive forces of desire, obtaining their return in the guise of an entirely satisfactory presence. Then it is the inextinguishable, increate real."[9] Char develops the question further (ibid., p. 200): "The poet must maintain an equal balance between the physical world of waking and the redoubtable ease of sleep; the lines of knowledge in which he couches the subtle body of the poem move indistinctly from one to the other of these different states of life."

Thus we have two complementary series of new relations: one between elements of the real—perceived differently because combined differently (Valéry); the other, between two existential states of the subject, the unconscious and the conscious, that comes alive in their contact with the real (Char). In this kind of *entrée en jeu* it is the concrete creative activity that pushes "rational contents, or contents dominated rationally, toward the secret and really biological irrationality of forms."[10]

Let us turn now to the complex network of contacts with the real that lie behind the text. When the poet enters the game on the side of meaning, the intersection of stimuli and lines of force produce in the text a result that can be objectively defined as a deviation from the common *grammar of vision*. By grammar of vision I mean the ensemble of perceptions, of ordinary associations, of traditions, of semiological codes, that are activated whenever anybody looks at something: in brief, the glance of the social subject. The poet is the person who escapes that grammar of vision, who does not follow its laws and classifications. As Pasternak says: "Only the passionate ardor of the elect can transform into poetry this 'truth that oppresses us with its laws'" (in Jakobson, 1973, p. 131). The poet, in changing his point of view and its level of intensity, substitutes for our habitual relations within the real other, new, and secret relations, and discovers unexpected contiguities or unusual ways of associating things, of substitutions. This reading of the real produced by what Char would call *énergie dislocante* (dislocating energy) generates the *productive knowledge of the real*.

Since no figural or symbolic operation exists in poetry outside of language, the poet's deviation from the normal grammar of vision takes the form of a violation of the norms of the grammar of the language. Coseriu makes an interesting distinction between system and norm in asserting that there are works that do not violate the grammar of language but still do not seem "normal," while Van Dijk has attempted to individualize the specifically artistic.[11] Baudelaire naturally can permit himself to go further; for him grammar is transformed into a magical evocation, losing "the purely relational character that constitutes its *aridity*—it degrammaticalizes itself."[12]

Lotman calls this process "the elimination of the prohibitions that exist on the level of natural language, prohibitions that prevent our joining elements inside the same semantic unity (inside the same word or inside the union of the sentence)."[13] It seems to me that it is already in the pre-text phase that the distinction seems to arise between poetic texts predominantly oriented toward the metonymic or toward the metaphoric; in this phase the "figures" appear in their generative force.[14]

It is a mirror-imaging process until the poet *yields the initiative to words,* as Mallarmé says,[15] and the *entrée en jeu* is provoked by a word, a rhythm, a phonic-timbric series that moves restlessly in search of a meaning. Perhaps no one characterized this pre-textual phase better than Mandelstam: "The verses live . . . in that sonorous echo of form that precedes written poetry. There is still not one word, and yet the verses already resound."[16] Elsewhere he speaks of "signal-waves," of "signaletic nets," so that it seems possible to recognize the existence in the poet of an *imagination of sounds,* that is, of a process of the imagination generated by sounds. Then the *combinaison des mots* magnetizes a meaning, and the hyperdetermination moves from the grammar of language to that of vision.

The subtle and stubborn self-imposition of a word has been the leitmotif of many poetic reflections on the pre-textual phase. Here is Gottfried Benn: "There is in fact something that can be called the way in which words arrange themselves around an author. Perhaps on that certain day he had come up against a certain word that preoccupied him, excited him, that he believed he could use as a leading motif."[17] Montale also says that often the incubation of a poem involves carrying a word around inside for a long time, conscious of its phonic weight, and that the poet does not yet know to what combinatorial game he will subject it. Mario Luzi also confirms this phenomenon in his description of the process by which a current word ceases, suddenly, to be a mere counter, and begins to signify.[18] It is then linked to other words until a "circuit" is born. Mandelstam again: "The living word does not define an object, but changes freely, almost at its own bidding, this or that objective significance, an exteriority, a dear body. And around the object the word wanders freely, like the soul around an abandoned but not forgotten body."[19]

From what the producers of poetry have told us, it always turns out that the "poetic" resists the impure flow of language-as-vehicle (Alfonso Gatto speaks of an *athletic poetic*) and creates necessary phonic-rhythmic or semantic links that would be arbitrary in normal language. It follows that in the nonliterary text, the semantic unity creates the link, while in the poetic text it is the link that creates the semantic unity. Klinkenberg, in the wake of S. Marcus, distinguishes between the *continuum* of meanings in poetry and the *discrete character* of meanings elsewhere in language.[20] Thus, what is "proper" to poetry—its otherness, *its legitimate strangeness*[21]—is precisely what is improper in common language.

Mallarmé and Valéry have clearly shown that, after the inception of the work, with its double *entrée en jeu*, there follows—in the phase of the work in progress (which already involves critical distancing)—a constant oscillation. This oscillation is a kind of counterdance between the universe of the signifiers and that of the signified. These universes act like complementary ensembles; and both the signifier and the signified claim equal rights in the achieved text. Andrea Zanzotto would say that in the oscillatory process the initial unity of the psyche is reconstituted. But this is a problem that reaches beyond an examination of the generative structure of the text and would require research of another nature. What interests us here is the moment in which constructive science is grafted onto invention.

Mallarmé continues: "But what is the use of the wonder of transposing a fact of nature in its almost oscillatory disappearance in word play, were it not that, out of the word play, there emanates, without the constraint of near or concrete recall, the pure notion. I say: a flower! And, beyond the forgetfulness to which my voice relegates any contour, there arises musically, and as something other than familiar calyxes, the idea itself, fragrant, and absent from all bouquets" (1945, p. 368). With this flower, which begins as a *fact of nature*, is subject to *almost oscillatory disappearance in word play*, and finally, absent from all *bouquets,* emerges as *pure notion,* Mallarmé illuminates for us the existence of an abstracting process, not achieved and not achievable by the route of logic, but only by way of the poetic. That flower, absent from all bouquets, can be taken as an emblem of the hypersignedness of poetry, the final outcome of language as sound that produces knowledge (see below, section 3).

Emphasizing the poet's double *entrée en jeu* in the generative process of the text has two results. On the one hand, it raises the question of a poetic linguistic competence—a competence which turns out to be of a different qualitative level from that of the nonartist, for the poet discovers a potentiality in language open to him alone. In addition, this capacity creates a series of underground tunnels that allow for the contact of linguistic elements that are ordinarily mutually inaccessible; and finally, it eliminates the arbitrariness of the sign. On the other hand, the input phase illuminates the output, that is, the production of the text. If what Agosti says is true for all poetic texts, if "in poetry, sense turns on itself, it confirms indefinitely and infinitely an initial hypostasis through the *vertical* distance that it accomplishes,"[22] then each different *entrée en jeu* can, as will be seen, leave traces of itself in the text.

Many students of poetic language, and especially Pagnini, have shown the outcome of the poetic production of meaning: the semantization of sounds, the semantization of syntax, the further semantization of the lexical meanings of language, the possible semantization of graphic aspects. Pagnini concludes: "The phases indicated take in the two typical poetic phenomena of the 'semantization of form' and of the 'slippage of the signified.'"[23] Nevertheless, this does not exclude the possibility that there are texts in which the level of the semantization of the signifiers is dominant and others in which the slippage of the signified is dominant. I am in accord with Lotman when he asserts that if a text does not suggest on one or some of its levels a partially traditional structure, but violates the structure of language altogether, its innovations would no longer be perceived. Riffaterre (1960) reaches conclusions like those of Lotman, conclusions that refer to the same level of the text, the stylistic level. He lets us see that the effect of unpredictability in any stylistic datum grows out of the high level of predictability in the context that precedes it, which does not have stylistic markers. In such cases, the effect of stylistic deviations overflows and overruns the previously unmarked traits, and gives those deviations a stylistic function.

If in some texts the semantization of the signifiers is dominant and in others the slippage of the signified, then the genesis of the kind of textual organization here schematized has, among its motivations, the model of the poet's *entrée en jeu* which characterizes the pre-text phase.

Among those studies that emphasize the equivalence of the formal elements as a dominant function, that of Agosti in Italy stands out. In his *Messagi formali*[24] he has examined different transsentential formal structures in various poets, such as the "rhythmic-timbric dynamic," the setting up of "phonetic figures," the production of "rhythmic and material objects," the "expansion of the signifier," and its dissemination. Serpieri's study of T.S. Eliot, by contrast, finds textually dominant features in a few semantic nuclei or profound images, obscurely generative, that preside over the production of the entire oeuvre of Eliot: "Naturally the individuation of the generative nuclei must not be static and definitive, but dynamic and provisional, so that we are urged to make innumerable excursions into the text to verify the solidarity of the sign-structures in the network of meanings."[25] Even allowing for the different deployment of the reader when he functions as critic, a deployment that orients each reading like a compass, it seems evident that, in the pre-textual phase, one of the two complementary ensembles—the formal and the semantic—acts as the dominant generative force. Starobinski, in his introduction to Char,[26] seems to be alluding to the pre-textual phase when he speaks of an *aldiquà* of poetry that exists alongside its *aldilà*, an *aldiquà* that "the energy of the poem never stops shaping."

## 3. THE HYPERSIGN FUNCTION OF THE POETIC TEXT

The importance of Jakobson's distinction between the six functions of language is well known. Equally well known is his definition of the poetic function, which "projects the principle of equivalence from the axis of selection into the axis of combination."[27] A fundamental consequence of this function would be that the role of poetic language is to communicate itself. In his essay, "*Roman Jakobson poéticien*,"[28] Todorov illustrates the growth of this concept (in Novalis, Mallarmé, the Russian Futurists) and emphasizes the temporal development of Jakobson's theoretical constructions; after 1960 Jakobson is intent not only on the phonic-rhythmic structures, but on the semantic structures of the grammar of poetry, a development of his original viewpoint which sees the poetic function as endowed with the power to render the referential function ambiguous. However, there seems to be one question which is still unclarified in Jakobson's theory: where is the qualitative difference between the application of the poetic function in language and the poetic language of a text? On a theoretical level, the two facts do not now seem coextensive (see IIIa.1), and neither do they seem so when we examine texts. A gross but rather instructive borderline case comes to mind: in the most sophisticated sector of Italian advertising, texts have recently appeared that are formally poetic and have been studied by Sabatini.[29] In these advertisements one can note grammatical figures, parallelisms, iterations, antitheses, complex rhetorical structures, rhyme—all the supposedly constitutive elements of the so-called grammar of poetry. There is a strong and informed use of the poetic function of language, but there is no poetry; poetry remains outside of and alien to this language.

Two reflections emerge from this borderline case: in the first place, as S.R. Levin has noted, every true poetic text generates a *special* code that has a unique message—the poetry itself.[30] That is to say, in poetry everything on the phonic and semantic level is pertinent, everything "signifies." Secondly, the trans-sentential unity of signifiers and meanings produces a global meaning of the text that is not absolutely the sum of the partial meanings isolable among them; our use of partial meanings is neutralized by the textual law, the law by which language undergoes a real metamorphosis. We are here in the presence of a hypersemantics that pertains only to the autonomy of poetic language and differentiates it qualitatively from every other type of language—including poetic advertising—in which the poetic function of language is used.

Let us take as an example the well-known phenomenon of the polysemy which characterizes poetic texts. It seems indispensable to distinguish between micropolysemy and macropolysemy; the first lives on the level of the single word, of the syntagm, of the styleme, which because of a particular semantic density become polyvalent. Thus Mandelstam defines the poetic word: "Every word is a bundle of meanings that, rather than converging at the same official point, irradiate in diverse directions";[31] that is, the density of the poetic word implies not only an exceptional sign-production but an irradiation—a flux of irradiating energy. Micropolysemy is the object of linguistic and critical-semiological research, whereas macropolysemy, the new sign-production of the text as such, is the special object of semiological criticism.

The text as a whole thus functions as a hypersign.[32] In reading *L'infinito* of Leopardi one notices—at the risk of stating the obvious—that the total meaning is not the sum of the meanings of the words and their enunciations—because the prime meaning, tied in some way to referents and pseudoreferents, is submerged as an incompatible and unconciliated element in the semantic organization of the poetic discourse. This also happens on the formal levels; for example, Brioschi, studying the framing metrical structure of *L'infinito*, concludes that it serves "the same function that the hill or the hedge play in the mental itinerary here undertaken: the form is nothing other than the starting point for an exploration of the unformed. The metric-

syntactic structures reproduce that same itinerary."[33] So it seems that the argument that poetic language communicates only itself, does not exhaust the question; it is valid only in that poetic language is autonomous with respect to its referents, that is, on the level of a primal semantics or the semantics of ordinary language. More precisely, the poetic text emits a message that changes the grammar of vision of its readers in the face of reality. We speak of hypersign and not of a secondary semantic because this latter notion may refer to the global aspect of every text—even the nonliterary text (and it would seem that even here, the whole is never the sum of its parts)—and to possible paraphrases of literary texts. (Suggestive examples were presented recently by R. Posner at a meeting held in Urbino, Italy, in July 1975 dedicated to metalanguage.)

## 4. THE GRAMMAR OF POETIC COMPETENCE

The real addressee of poetic language is the person who, following the instructions of the text, crosses the threshold of the text's semantics and—in a process which inversely retraces that of the poet—partially recovers the pre-text phase. As Risset says: "The characteristic act of reading poetry is to let the mind descend from the agile surface of the words to the substance in which the essential moves, provoking in the mental rhythm a startling slowdown of the natural movement."[34] It has been said justly that the system of artistic information is very costly; if the volume of information were not remunerative, the reader would not submit to its cost. In the special relation between sender and addressee that the poetic text creates, there may be another confirmation of the qualitative difference of poetic competence: the poet's statements are not only new—a fact that is true for any speaker—but are incapable of substitution. They are not subject to extrapolation from the general context without the loss of the very possibility of poetic communication. In view of this, one might be tempted to speak, with Blanchot,[35] of the "miracle" of poetic reading, as of a *Lazare, veni foras;* but such a view unnecessarily runs the risk of making of us celebrators of epiphanies in a manner all too reminiscent of Idealist poetics. It is rather the complexity of the poetic object as a hypersign that I wish to insist upon. A better reference would be Umberto Eco in his recent *A Theory of Semiotics,* in which he is concerned with the semiotic elements of the artistic text in general: ". . . the esthetic text represents a sort of summary and laboratory model of all the aspects of sign-function; it can perform any or all productive functions, being composed of various types of judgment and acting as a *metasemiotic statement.*"[36] Again, "The esthetic text acquires the *status* of a *supersign-function* that correlates correlations."[36a]

I should like to add that just as in the *entrée en jeu* in the pre-text phase the sender is involved completely—consciously and unconsciously—so is the addressee involved. In other words, the formal structures of poetic language, the phonic-rhythmic series, the correlations of timbre and syntax are often "felt" by the reader more than they are rationally received. Such intuition leads to the subtle game of mirrors between the signifier and the signified. This accounts for the critical emphasis on the typology of poetic reception—an issue that must be added to those vaster problems (for which see IIb) of reading and decoding in general.

Today research is taking place on many levels, especially the mathematical, to find a grammar of poetic enunciations. Behind such research is the ambitious program of discovering a "poetic system" or poetic *langue.*[37] Bierwisch, for example, is looking for a *Selektionsmechanismus,* or "selection-mechanism," ($P^1$) that has as its input the structural description of the sentence in the poetic text (SB = *Strukturelle Beschreibung*). As its output, $P^1$ furnishes two classes, $SB^1$ and $SB^2$, in which $SB^1$ would only include structures which correspond to poetic rules. But Bierwisch himself has noted how, in order to function, $P^1$ must be the bearer of a finite system of rules capable of distinguishing poetic structures from all others. Therefore, by modifying $P^1$ in a way that allows for a better rapport between linguistic and poetic structure, he uses P to indicate the mechanism that can sort out the two series of enunciations according to gradations, and arrange them in succession on a scale of poeticality.

To the complex of rules that constitute P, for example, that rule of Jakobson's would apply in which the principle of equivalence moves from the axis of selection to the axis of combination. Such rules of P operate on linguistic enunciations, but evidently they are in themselves extralinguistic. But here the difficulty begins. Bierwisch maintains that poetics as a science must accept poetic effects as factual data and must only establish their functional rules. The objection arises: on the basis of what criteria is the "poetic scale" created and are the rules of deviation specified? Bierwisch maintains and insists that the deviations can be considered poetic only if founded on regularity; in other words, only if they are not arbitrary deviations. Things, however, are not so simple if Bierwisch himself feels obliged to reveal that "a fixed system of rules generally originates first with the work, in which it breaks down, so that it by no means exists as a given code" (Bierwisch, 1969, p. 61). Thus one often notes the fact that a given system of rules has for its realization a unique text that embodies its own code, so that the reader, as Bierwisch says, finds himself "in the situation of the cipher-analyst, who does not decode, but must break the code." It seems very significant that Bierwisch, apropos of the microstructure of a single text, is finally in accord with Contini on the *pertinence* within the poetic text even of an exceptional and unique form.

At this point we may conclude that the work of Bierwisch, like that of other scholars, is valid when directed toward a catalogue of rules of poetic pertinence, that is, the rules referable to the new functional character that linquistic elements assume within literary and poetic structures (see also Doležel, 1966). It becomes the project for a sort of grammar of poetic competence; or as Van Dijk would have it, a *competence-system* and *performance-system* (see IIIa.1) referable to literary language understood diachronically and synchronically—a study complementary to that of general rhetoric and style. The current tendency toward generalization, however, must not make us forget that just as, in the narrative artifice of defamiliarization, the habitual and usual becomes new and surprising through the unfamiliar point of view, so do poetic enunciations become deviant through the intervention of the sublimely defamiliarizing artifice that is the complex interaction of all levels—the principle or individual law of the text.

## 5. LANGUAGE AS SELF-COMMUNICATION

In a typology of poetic texts we must keep in mind that there are texts about which we can rightly say that poetic language communicates only itself, that is, its own material reality and its own organization. For example, Zumthor extrapolates from certain medieval texts a language that "makes reference only to itself," where "the ensemble of potential signifiers of the thing is substituted for the name of the thing to be discovered,"[38] a language that itself speaks in conformity with specific poetics (including the limit cases of artificial poetic languages in which to poeticize becomes an operation analogous to chess). But more complex is the case of the Carolingian *carmina figurata*, where the verses are constructed so that they contain letters in fixed places, letters which, when linked together, yield a hidden meaning in the poem. Besides this, the lines generated by these letters create a geometric design or an emblematic image; such iconographic writing is itself a text "integrated in the poetic macrotext, indissolubly linked to it by the signifying materiality of the letters; it is meaning, and the most profound meaning, that this architecture of signs conceals."[39]

In modern times, some appropriate examples of language that speaks itself come from texts of the literary avant-garde, which present themselves as "the provisional emergence of an operation that is then redone,"[40] as work on the linguistic

functioning of the text, as premeditated murders of the signified, as the surrender to a provisional negation of the face of
the world. In this kind of poetry, the signifiers eliminate the
signified in conformity with a poetic of noncommunication
or—as was the modish way of putting it a few years ago in
certain militant cultural circles—a poetic of the "communication of a noncommunication."

## 6. THE POETIC TEXT IN PROGRESS; THE STATUTE OF THE VARIANTS

Between the pre-text and the completed poetic text, the
different phases of execution are situated; this is the area of
variants or of the convertibility of the poetic material—the most
indomitable and, in the end, the most "exact" of all materials.
In this interval, long or short as it may be, the "artifice" that
forges and re-creates the forms is set in motion. Around this
"artifice" two antithetical conceptions circle—and reach definition.

On the one hand, the poet at this stage is like Poe, who sees
in this process of producing variants something that is aimed at
attaining the "ultimate point of completion."[41] This idea is
found again in Gottfried Benn: "Here is the mystery: the poem
is already finished before it begins; only the poet does not yet
know the text. The poem absolutely cannot be different from
what it then is, when it is finished. You know exactly when it is
finished, but naturally the process can go on for a long time, for
weeks, for years, but before it is finished, you do not let it go."
From such a perspective, the labor of corrections is strictly
bound to the necessity of rendering the text as it "must" be.

On the other hand, there is the conception expressed by
Mallarmé and Valéry and adopted by our greatest student of
the variant-process, Gianfranco Contini; they see poetry as "an
unending approximation to value."

Valéry, as we know, was able to imagine a topography of
variants: "Perhaps it would be interesting to construct a work

*once* that would show in each of its *knots* the diversity that can there present itself to the mind; in that diversity the mind might *choose* the unique follow-through that will appear in the text. That would substitute for the illusion of a unique decision, imitative of the real, a decision *possible at each instant,* which seems to me more true."[42] Contini, in his *Saggio d'un commento alle correzioni del Petrarca volgare* of 1942 says: "The poetic school that began with Mallarmé and has in Valéry its own theoretician, considering poetry under the aegis of its making, interprets poetry as a perennially mobile and unfinishable activity, in which the historic poem represents a possible—and strictly speaking, gratuitous—section, and not necessarily the ultimate section. It is a point of view of the producer, not of the user. However, if the critic understands the work of art as an 'object,' which represents only the objectivity of his [own critical] operations, that 'datum' is the moral working hypothesis of his [the critic's] own abnegation. And a consideration of the poetic *act* will lead the critic to shift his formulas dynamically, to discover the directions, rather than the fixed contours of poetic energy. Authorial corrections are best described as directives and not as boundaries."[43]

Poe has written suggestively on the correcting activity itself, behind which lie the psychological situations, events, and self-encounters of the poet: and he has enumerated "the innumerable glimpses of idea that arrived not at the maturity of full view—at the fully matured fancies discarded in despair as unmanageable—at the cautious selections and rejections—at the painful erasures and interpolations—in a word, at the wheels and pinions—the tackle for scene-shifting—the stepladders and demon traps—the cock's feathers, the red paint and the black patches, which, in ninety-nine cases out of the hundred, constitute the properties of the literary *histrio.*"[43a] Naturally, Poe's description is equally valid for poetic and prose texts, and also involves problems in the structural organization of the work (see IV.1). What concerns us here is the gradual adjustment of the poetic language of a text through the dynamics of variants, for they are prime moments in the formal structuring of the work and illuminate the very nature of poetic writing—that writing in which, in a certain way, everything is everywhere.

Contini offers us illuminating examples of poetic procedures in his examination of the variants in Petrarch and Leopardi;[44] to the dynamic of the poetic *act*, he adds the dynamic of the critic's work, and important theoretical considerations emerge from this addition. First, he recognizes that "shifts are shifts in a system, and therefore involve a multitude of connections with the other elements of the system and with the entire linguistic culture of the reviser." This system seems to be associated with what we have identified above (section 3) as the constructive laws of the text, or as its dynamic equilibrium. The "linguistic culture of the reviser" is the place of possible choices, the paradigmatic ground of language and above all of literary language (the sphere of synonyms, and of potentiality of phonic-timbric or semantic associations). What seems important here is the reflection that in the final phases of reelaboration (final in praxis, even if in theory no definitive text exists), the last chosen version is no longer in a dynamic relation with other possible versions; we can say that in a certain sense the text has achieved its closure. In fact, Contini, after having followed the variant-process of Sonnet CXCVII of Petrarch, concludes: "The rhythmic period has been closed. For as much as is possible for a mobile perfection, especially for the mobile in Petrarch, the click of the spring—of which Alain speaks—has taken place. It would be difficult to reopen this lock" (Contini, 1970, p. 12). For such admirable closures Alfonso Gatto uses the expression "victory after the struggle." Because it really is a struggle: poets give abundant evidence of the resistance the text makes during the work of revision, presenting itself in some way as a void, a split, an absence of equilibrium that may persist for a long time only to be resolved mysteriously in an instant, a happy, unforeseen instant: that is where the intersubjectivity of the author comes into play, the discourse of the Other that intersects with that of consciousness. As Char has noted: "In poetry, it is only with communication and the free disposition of the totality of things among themselves through us that we find ourselves engaged and defined, able to obtain our original form and our probative properties."[45]

Returning to Contini, who notes that in Petrarch two movements coalesce in the variant-process: "one is a movement of ideas (but also of tone), the other is a pure movement of tone,"[46] we can deduce from this (apart from a possible correlation with our initial view of the poet's pre-textual double *entrée en jeu*) the principle of vital interaction among the levels that constitute the poetic text. This interaction can reach isomorphism, even if from time to time in practice the semantic level or, alternatively, the phonic level takes on a dominant role. Examples of these levels occur in Leopardi, as in *percorrea la faticosa tela* (XXI, 22) where *percorrea* was substituted for *percotea*. [Line 22 of the poem, *A Silvia*, says that Silvia's "swift hand *(man veloce)* ran across *(percorrea)*" the loom, while the earlier variant, *"percotea,"* means "it struck."—A.M.] Having identified the Virgilian influence (from *percurrens pectine telas*) in the variant Leopardi substituted, Contini acutely adds that in this correction "there remains a very mysterious margin: does the phonic proximity of the two versions indicate, perhaps, that *percorrea* was intentionally immanent in *percotea*, that *percotea* is a first associative approximation—although blurred—of the mental object?"[47] The best comment on such an observation as Contini's is put forth metaphorically by Mandelstam: "The indestructibility of the foul copy is a dynamic law of the work of art. To reach the goal one must gather the contrary wind and exploit it: this is precisely the tacking procedure that any sailing ship must observe."[48]

The tactics of the combinatorial game in the process of correction or of new collocations are amply described in Contini's critical work: contiguous or distant compensations, changes in register, a prevalent tendency toward certain choices (Leopardi's preference for *vago* as against *dolce*) starting from a base of bilateral equilibrium, retouchings with the intent of interiorizing the text, double operations on the stylemes of literary language (overarching or recovering them), phonic or semantic associations, etc.—as well as behavior that varies in accord with the metric genre.

The gradual realization of the poetic text, through a dynamic of variants that are always correlated in proximity or at a distance, proves the transsentential unity of the text at the level of the signifiers and the signified. But it also confirms that only an exceptional use of that kind of language, its ascension toward an architectonically based optimum state, can reach the highest level of the sign-function of literary language. The Horatian theme of the metamorphosis of the poet seems to have spanned the centuries; and it is still meaningful, still felicitous. That is why poetic language has been treated so specifically in this chapter.

# IV. Hypersign

## 1. THE CONSTRUCTIVE PROCESS OR THE WILL OF THE WORK

Every study of a work of art requires a working hypothesis and a coherent perspective. But perspectives are multiple and complementary—and though this makes for their relative character, it also makes for their operative value. The character of a hypothesis is relative in that every theoretical or experimental approach leaves something "untranslated" in the work, and the value of a hypothesis is operative in that our goal is not to find an ontological solution but to reduce our losses of that in the text which cannot be translated into critical discourse. The term "hypersign," used here for the work of art considered in its semiological perspective, attests to the fact that the work can produce a high yield of information precisely because the work-as-a-whole strengthens the complex of its constituent signs. This question has already been discussed in IIIb in regard to the hypersemantics of the poetic text.

From the point of view of the sender or producer of the artistic message, there are writers for whom the work is born out of a more or less unitary idea, so that the author sees the generative structure of the text with a certain clarity from the beginning. And on the contrary, there are authors for whom the structuring process is realized through successive phases of redimensioning and transformations. In the latter case, it is the constructive function *in act* that motivates the transformations; the work in progress dictates its own laws, in a certain sense it

imposes its will on the author. In another context I have noted
the singular comment made by Thomas Mann on a letter that
Wagner sent to Liszt (20 November 1851) apropos of the
genesis of the *Ring of the Nibelung:*

> And then he recounts this extraordinary story, for him so unex-
> pected, so wonderful, so happy! One must hear him recount it in
> his own words to understand how little an artist knows, in the
> beginning, of his work; how poorly he knows the obstinacy of
> the being that he has to deal with, how little he divines what the
> work wants, what his work must—precisely because it is his
> work—become. In the face of his work, he very often finds him-
> self in the state of mind that expresses itself in the words: "I did
> not want this, but now I must. God help me." The ardent ambi-
> tion of the I does not exist at the beginning of great works, not at
> their origins. The ambition is not of the artist, but of the work-
> . . . that imposes its will on him.[1]

A more recent testimony, beautiful in its succinct clarity, is that
of Gabriel García Márquez talking about his latest novel, *The
Autumn of the Patriarch:*

> Then, with *One Hundred Years of Solitude* completed, finding my-
> self in Barcelona, I took up again the manuscript of *The Autumn of
> the Patriarch* and began to write what I believed would be the
> definitive version. But little by little the entire technical concep-
> tion that I had thought through about how the story was to be
> recounted, changed, even as I was writing it. I ended up throw-
> ing everything away and I rewrote it several times from the be-
> ginning. And that is how it took seven years. In other words, I
> gradually learned how to write this novel as I wrote it.[2]

These two passages lead us to reflect on the fact that the
initial freedom of the writer in the face of the ideation of a work
is destined to diminish, to encounter limits as the physiognomy
of the work takes on concrete lineaments and imposes itself on
the author. It is perhaps the only process in which a lessening
of freedom constitutes a positive, efficient element on the level
of invention. No one is more instructive on this subject than
Poe; in *The Philosophy of Composition*,[3] he illustrates the *modus*

*operandi*—however polemically emphasized—of an author and the progressive generation of a structure: little by little, as the poet selects themes, motifs, images, rhythms, meter, his previous choices allow him fewer alternative possibilities, until at the end the structure is sturdy as iron, exactly the case of *The Raven*. If alternative possibilities lessen as the constructive process develops (see IIa.4), then it follows that meaningful "absence," on a thematic or formal level, belongs rather to the phases of genesis than to the successive phases, where that which is absent can no longer count as heavily as that which is present.

Naturally the problem of the successive structuring of a work must not be confused with the problem of its different versions. A writer who realizes the physiognomy and organization of a work through arduous labor is also inclined to reworking and rewriting; but this is simply another confirmation of the travail of construction. An example is the difficult rapport of Jacobo Sannazaro with his most famous work, *Arcadia*.[4] Starting with a faith in the code of the bucolic genre that leads him to loosely linked eclogues, Sannazaro arrives at a new idea—and this idea must have been immediate and unhesitating—a new structure: prose alternating with the eclogues and serving as a frame, a lyric background in which to set the eclogues. The novelty is already striking: a structure proper to the didactic-allegoric romance is transferred to the bucolic genre. But evidence of the constructive process is revealed at about the middle of *Arcadia*; there, to use Mann's image, the work begins to offer resistance, to dictate its will to the author, revealing to him the necessity for transforming the initial generative structure. It is as if in the beginning the novelty of the prose-poetry complex had not been seen by the author with all its intrinsic possibilities of innovative development. Beginning with Prose VI the center of gravity changes: the exclusively lyric prose undergoes alterations and is modified slowly but inexorably toward narrative; the descriptive monody of the earlier prose portions gives way to the stylistic polyphony of the tale. The romantic pastoral, unforeseen at the beginning of the work, is now born; and the poetic texts, now completely changed in function, come to serve as comment, as lyric integration. The architectonic structure is changed; and with it, not only the prose-poetry relation, but the correlation of all levels of the text, the system of isotopes, is changed. One witnesses the transformation that the narrative, novelistic element produces on the bucolic themes as they turn from pastoral pictures into the dynamic forms of the tale. To schematize: (1) the person who says "I" assumes the dominant role; (2) a narrative line develops, consisting of that person and his story; (3) a mythic universe gives way to the universe of memory, to a precise temporal category; (4) to the temporal category there is joined the spatial category: real and definite places; (5) chain reactions are engendered—the pastoral characters are no longer interchangeable but stand in different, specific relationships with the principal actor.

To the fundamental changes in the form of the content—the organization of the thematic-symbolic levels—there corresponds a change in the form of expression on the syntactic-stylistic levels (the new syntactic architecture) and on the lexical and rhythmic levels.

At least two deductions of a general nature follow: two diverse generative structures underlie the first and second part of *Arcadia*, and the second of these structures has asserted itself in an advanced phase of the work's construction. More revolutionary than the first, the second part has called into question the very codification of the bucolic genre, which has now been transformed into another genre, the pastoral romance. Another deduction: the second generative structure has produced a coaxial shift of all the thematic and formal levels of the text, and this confirms the principle of isomorphism and interlevel isotopy, whose sphere of action in the literary hypersign is vast (IV.2)—even if it is not exclusive and total. The case of Sannazaro's *Arcadia* is exceptionally instructive; for, paradoxically, we are facing two texts linked in one work and written in a rather short period—1483–1485. It is as if a new structural principle has guided the writer as he worked with syntactic-stylistic and rhythmic deviations occurring as the form of the contents deviated: it has led him to a new formal statute. To conclude this discussion on the continuous role change between author and work we can say, on the one hand, with Gottfried Benn, that the work is like the ship of the Phaecians, of which Homer tells us that it enters directly into port without the need of a pilot;[5] on the other hand, we are searching here for the exact elements and serviceable clues that will yield an appropriate enough image of the process of construction by the author.

## 2. LEVELS OF THE TEXT

The literary work, whether in prose or poetry, is constructed on several levels. That these levels—thematic, symbolic, ideological, stylistic or discursive, morphosyntactic, lexical, phonic-timbric, rhythmic, metric—are to be related is a fact so accepted from the time of the Russian Formalists to the present as to be considered a constant of modern thought and critical activity. More recent, and still in an investigative theoretical phase, is the distinction between the surface structure of the work, where the interaction of different levels takes place, and the deep structure or macrostructure to which we owe the coherence of the text, its constitutive law. Van Dijk, who is concerned with this problem,[6] rightly observes that a coherent macrostructure may manifest itself in the text through discontinuous local microstructures. It is precisely the analyses of these latter that show how the apparently incoherent finds its coherence either in transsentential and interlevel groupings or in the deep macrostructure.

To extrapolate and study textual levels separately with the purpose of then placing them in relationship to each other is an inevitable violence wrought by the analytic praxis of the critic on the compositional unity of the work on its syntagmatic level. The compensation lies in being able at the end to grasp the organizing law of the text and, above all, its dynamic nature, which certainly is not implicit in the formalizing concept of deep macrostructure. As we know, the various levels can be related horizontally or vertically; in the first are grouped the functional unities belonging to the continuum on the same level. Critical modes actually exist that are defined by the specific level on which they concentrate: stylistic criticism, symbolic criticism, sociological criticism, etc. On the second, vertical plane the interlevel linkings take place. Pagnini speaks of *horizontal and vertical isotopy*.[7]

However, we must add a postscript to what has been said and what will be said: the current neoenlightenment tendency to study the structure of a work must not be confused with the confidence of being able to explain everything, that is to assign all functions to the structure. In every authentic creation there is something that Borges would call *in flight*, asymmetrical, decentered, directed toward spaces that are indicated but not made explicit by the text. This may explain in part why no author would ever declare a work of his *definitive*. Besides, in the name of discontinuous structures there may appear "places" of deviation in the text from the relations of homology and isomorphism between its levels—places in which the split, the break, the hole indicate that something especially important is happening. The search for a perfect interlevel correspondence that excludes the asymmetrical activities of the text runs the risk of producing a constricting grid—a grid for which not the writer but the analytic critic, in his desire for a harmonizing vision of the reality of the text, is responsible.

Returning now to the question of the vertical direction, to what is produced on the different levels of the work, perhaps a greater clarity and order can be achieved by analogy, by reference to the relational modes that logicians and mathematicians build between the elements of two or more sets: the relation of one-to-one, one-to-many, many-to-one, many-to-many. While the possibility of one-to-one relations seems to be excluded, since no literary text exists in which the unities of one level (1,2,3,4,5, etc.) correspond one-to-one to the unities of another level (a,b,c,d,e, etc.), the one-to-many relation can illuminate the concept of a dominant level. It is that level which, because of its influence, causes the elements of the other levels to move in a certain direction. For example, let us take a text belonging to the well-codified medieval genre of the *débat* or disputation: the *Disputatio rosae cum viola* of Bonvesin de la Riva. In an earlier analysis by me of this text, to which the reader can refer,[8] I was able to show how a binary opposition arising on the symbolic level makes that level dominant; in that case a one-to-many relation takes place between the binary generative structure of the symbolic level and its realizations on the various other levels of the text. On the obviously subordinated thematic level, the opposition rose-violet will be produced; on the stylistic level there will be a series of microstructures linked through constant, repeated parallelisms and antitheses, with strong consequences on the rhetorical level; in addition, antithetical blocks will organize the syntactic series with strong phonic-rhythmic implications. The strophic organization is in its turn heavily determining the opposing syntactic blocks. Obviously, we do not always have occasion to deal with texts of such explicit and harmonizing construction—they are a little like artistic "official" buildings in the country of literature.

As for the many-to-many relation, it may be readily studied as long as the unities of one level correspond *en masse* to a series on another level. A typical example is the relation between syntactic series and rhythmic series in prose and poetry, between phonic-timbric and rhythmic series in poetry—series that involve a chain of orderly repetition. In such cases, the eventual noncorrespondence of the series—for instance, in enjambment in poetry, where metric and syntactic structures diverge—is a phenomenon that assumes a semantic function and actually becomes evident through the deviation from the norm of the text. This happens because of the fact that in the reading and reception of the text the levels are perceived simultaneously. Thus in a modern lyric written without rhyme, the presence of a few sporadic rhymes is a significant example of asymmetry, a symptom or connotation of something that must be explained at another textual level. As always, deviations have meaning only in relation to that which follows the normative way. As Zamjatin would say: "To jump high, to detach oneself from the earth it is necessary that this earth exist" (Zamjatin, p. 46).

From this vantage point the examination of variants is most interesting. For example, in *La Madonna dei filosofi*, a story by Gadda, one can see how the substituted syntactic variants are conditioned by the emergence of a new rhythm that is given an always more privileged status by the author.[9] A many-to-many relation between the narrative level and the syntactic level (verb tenses) has been studied by Segre in an essay called "Structures and Registers in the *Fiammetta*."[10] That text of Boccaccio presents a perfect correspondence between the blocks of elements of one level and those of another, as the following table shows:

|      | Narrative Time        | Verbal Tense          |
|------|-----------------------|-----------------------|
| I    | progressive           | perfect               |
| II   | progressive           | perfect               |
| III  | mental                | imperfect             |
| IV   | mental                | imperfect             |
| V    | progressive mental    | perfect and imperfect |
| VI   | progressive           | perfect               |
| VII  | progressive           | perfect               |
| VIII | presentative          | present               |
| IX   | desiderative          | imperative            |

Naturally, the more artistically complex the text, the more the individual types of interaction of levels are embedded in the development of the entire textual discourse, where the great combinatorial game of stylistic registers takes place. Apropos of the *Fiammetta*, Segre shows how the organized alternation of stylistic registers is "a stylistic correlation, not a representation, of a topical sentimental event and of a range of states of mind that give the topic variety." There is, therefore, a strict interaction between a psychological level with many valences and the corresponding stylistic level, which is so constructed as to bring out by homology the valences themselves.

The recent works of Agosti, Tavani, and Beccaria[11] on the levels marked by the power of the signifier in poetic texts—the phonic-timbric, rhythmic, and metric—reveal complex situations in which the autonomy possible on one level is complemented by its interaction with other levels. Three typical results can be sketched here:

I.   The formal, phonic-timbric, and rhythmic figures are independent of the textual meanings and do not serve as carriers of equivalents of the contents.[12]

II.   The formal figures occur in correlation with meaning. Here Beccaria says:

> The signifier in poetry is disengaged from its strictly linguistic function and renews the word as a sort of symbol; it gives the word a fringe of sense that touches less the intellect, the linguistic-communicative operations, and more the sensibility, the unconscious, the preverbal, the noncommunicable mental contents; the orchestration, the poetic score, the "tuned" *iunctura*, the single word considered to be phonetically "motivated," can liberate, as in a sort of Freudian "regression," energies and latent associations; it can implicate concepts, mental contents, communicate the unknowable, reestablish an underlying harmony, as in an ancestral language (Mallarmé), with a language one no longer knows (Pascoli). . . . Only when the poet links the sound, arbitrarily, to a meaning do qualities emerge that ally that sound to that meaning and include that sound in the connotations of the meaning.[13]

III.   There are suprasegmental articulations of the signifier, especially demonstrated with fine critical acumen by Agosti, that produce semantic evasiveness and—therefore—true supplementary messages of a formal nature.[14] Thus, the text is codified several times, from which its hyperfunction as sign and communication.

## 3. POLES OF TENSION AND TRANSSENTENTIAL UNITY

There is something more in the richness of a text that, like life itself, has an abundant capacity for dissolving opposites. In fact, a serious inquiry into textual levels in both horizontal and vertical directions, while emphasizing isotopy and homology, also makes evident the contrasts that regulate the dynamics of single works. These two antithetical but coexistent movements are individuated by Egorov when he defines the literary text as "a field of forces similar to the electromagnetic or gravitational field with condensations and functional crossovers," where everything in some way is "reciprocally conditioned" through homology or by contrast.[15] The coincidence of similar ideas in Gadda is not casual: he refers to the *polar tension* "between the represented and the represented" or thematic material, a tension that involves the totality of the text.[16] Gombrich gives evidence of an analogous reality for the pictorial text: "Instead of a fairly simple parallelogram of psychological forces we are here confronted with the highest type of organization. Here we must assume countless pulls and counterpulls on a hierarchy of levels that would baffle analysis even if we had greater insight into the kind of elements used. Every inch of any painting in any style may testify to a yielding to regressive impulses in the color employed and to a domination of such impulse in the disciplined brushwork that husbands its force for the climax.

> . . . there is a dark
> Inscrutable workmanship that reconciles
> Discordant elements, makes them cling together
> In one society. . . ."[17]

We need the organic study of textual levels to be able to distinguish better between the phenomena of writing in prose and in poetry according to canons that complement the traditional ones (for example, by emphasizing the supplemental formal messages in poetry). We also need such study in order to call attention to what there is in common between the hypersign in poetry and prose, to that which links them both to the foundations of literary communication. We have already seen how, in examining the constructive complexity of the prose text, Zamjatin arrives at the notion that to be a prose master "is as difficult as completing an interplanetary voyage" (Zamjatin, p. 68). Whence the impossibility in prose or poetic texts of paraphrasing or transcodifying from the artistic system into nonartistic communication without a loss in information,[18] or of applying to literary texts the pure and simple results of the principles of textual linguistics valid for nonliterary texts, given the diverse nature of the *performance*.[19]

The organic study of levels can contribute something to a typology of prose. One example, almost a limit case, is the prose of Gadda, which is not only stupendous but particularly instructive for our purposes. In the introduction to *Cognizione del dolore*, the author declares that "the baroque and the grotesque already inhabit things, in the discrete discoveries of a phenomonology external to us: in the very expressions of custom, in the notions 'commonly' accepted by the few and the many: and in humanities or 'inhumanities' as they may be: grotesque and baroque not ascribable to a premeditated will or an expressive tendency of the author but linked to nature and to history . . . so that the habitual cry 'Gadda is baroque' can be commuted to the more reasonable and more quiet assertion, 'the world is baroque and Gadda has perceived and portrayed its baroqueness.'"[20] Everyone knows very well that in effect expressivity prevails over mimesis in Gadda and that his exceptional linguistic expressionism arises from the polar tension between "the represthe and the represented."

Now, if it is true that in Gadda, as in every great prose writer, the transsentential unity of the writing or of the work-as-a-whole as signifier corresponds to the rendering, on the level of thematic structure, of an interpretation of the world, then it is significant and even provocative to find that the existentially *asystematic* becomes *polysystematic* in the writing. Gadda himself says that this occurs through what he defines as "a reconstructive program, even if it is a program felt instinctively."[21] In the prose of Gadda, studied in slow motion, various linguistic codes (dialectal, technical, aulic, Latinizing, etc.) meet. These elements are held in balance on one or more levels by a general constructive force. These codes meet and clash according to the laws of the text, provoking a burst of surprises in the reader not accustomed to the connubiums of a heterogeneous style and its spastic use. Besides, part of the high quotient of information in Gadda's writing derives from the fact that the violations produced by the combinations of different codes proclaim horizontally, behind the syntagmatic level, the presence of different paradigmatic levels; but these codes intersect vertically with varying intensity so as to create reciprocally their own deformation. Thus the importance of relating the unities of all levels, from the phonic to the lexical, to capture the extraordinary polysystemic structure. The simile of the builder in the act of constructing, a simile dear to the writer, certainly is no accidental one. (And see note 21.)

From this limit case we can turn to one less dramatic. It is well known that in *Conversazione in Sicilia* by Elio Vittorini a lyric-evocative stylistic register corresponds to the thematic-symbolic and mythic levels. Vittorini's originality becomes vivid and suggestive if we focus on the dialogue. The change in function of the dialogue exchanges is clear, transferred as they are from the levels of representation or action, where they usually belong, to a level of lyric expansion in strict relation to the symbolic level. That is, the character-symbol is the spokesman of a "saying" that illuminates his symbolicness. The violations of a normal use of narrative dialogue in general do not take place on the lexical level but rather on the phonic-rhythmic and syntactic levels, which are constructed in perfect collaboration for a sort of ballet interwoven by their formal elements. This results in a conspicuously iterative structure with recurring phonic expansions, insistent parallelisms, anaphoric or epanaphoric sequences, rhythmic and atemporal parataxis. The lyric dialogue thus grows out of an internal coherence, and in a certain sense the form becomes the highest content.

On the horizontal plane the transsentential perspective, extended to the text as a whole, allows us to recover many elements of internal cohesion on the separate levels, including the so-called repetitions at a distance, the various formal traces of that "archive of memory" so masterfully consulted by Contini in the case of Dante. That is, the critic, by retracing in his inquiry the pathways of the various levels, can (and more easily than he can when he is confronting the completeness and complexity of the work) recognize and memorize those links between the single elements that orient the entire itinerary of a work; he can construct a memory common to both the author and himself (IIb.4).

## 4. THE SEMANTIC OF MANY STEPS

It was Tynjanov who first showed that one level can dominate in the construction of a work, but that it is also possible for different levels to rise to dominance in our use of the work. A robust *distinguo* is needed; on the one hand, it may happen that only the decoder is responsible for the hieratic reordering (cf. IIb and the problem of the various decodifyings), a phenomenon illustrated by this example from Eliot: "In a play of Shakespeare you get several levels of significance. For the simplest auditors there is the plot, for the more thoughful the character and conflict of character, for the more literary the words and phrasing, for the more musically sensitive the rhythm, and for the auditors of greater sensitiveness and understanding a meaning which reveals itself gradually."[22] Naturally, Eliot adds, a clear-cut classification of the public as an ensemble of decodifiers is impossible to contemplate, given the different levels of consciousness of that which is assimilated. He concludes that what counts is that no one is disturbed by the presence of what he does not understand, but stays with natural ease at the level or levels he has chosen. What does this mean? That the literary text, more than any other verbal text, is by its nature constructed in a manner that can offer different significative and communicative approaches. And this leads us to the other aspect, our use of the work, and so to the problem of literary communication, a problem of much greater importance from the point of view of semiology.

There are cases in which the ensemble of constitutive signs of a text is consciously organized by the author in order to express, on different structural levels, different messages—a stratified communication, so to speak. Lotman uses the phrase "semantic of many steps" in that the interlevel perspective changes according to the step to which the reading of the addressee rises, and consequently the communication changes. In similar complex types of texts "every particular and the whole text in its ensemble are included in diverse relational systems, and as a result, they assume contemporaneously more than one meaning."[23] Lotman chooses as an example the ancient *Sermon on Law and Grace* by the Metropolitan Hilarion; and he interprets this text in his usual masterly fashion, inserting also the notion of the ludic effect caused by the presence of various levels of meaning, which do not coexist statically, but "flashingly," "scintillating" inside the continuum of the discourse. We have here the fullest version of the macropolysemy of a literary text and the resulting pertinence of defining it as a hypersign.

Lotman first individuates the level of opposition of freedom-slavery; then through the meaning of new signs and a new reading of old signs, the level of opposition of Christianity-paganism; then the third step is reached, with the opposition of new-old to which is linked the antithesis grace-law. Finally, in the sociopolitical context of the age, there are the conflicting cultural visions of the court of Yaroslav and that of Byzantium.

In Italian literature an example corresponding to the *Sermon* would be the already cited *Disputatio rosae cum viola* by Bonve-

sin de la Riva, which also offers material for some specific implications of a theoretical nature.

The reader of the *Disputatio* is presented with a first, thematic
level in which two flowers are contrasted—the rose and the
violet. Bonvesin inherits from tradition the theme of two flowers in conflict, essential to the binary structure even if the final
presence of a judge presents a ternary conclusion to the text:
the dispute is settled by a judgment, that is, a form which is
metaphorically judicial.

To this thematic level there is added, according to the canons
of traditional allegory, a symbolic level organized in accord
with an ethical system that opposes vices and virtues. The rose
symbolizes lust, avarice, pride, the triad of the beasts of Dante,
while the violet symbolizes the corresponding virtues of chas-
tity, charity, humility. The relation between the two levels,
very explicit in the text, realizes the specific sign-function that
is conferred on the chosen objects, the two flowers, in the
highly symbolic medieval culture. The most usual reading of
the *Disputatio* as well as the re-creative process of literary communication have consisted in decodifying such antitheses.
Nevertheless, the text offers a series of indicators of the
possibility of a second symbolic level, of a new turn in the
reading, of an ulterior communication. Because we are dealing
with a medieval text, a citation by Lotman from the *Izbornik
Svjatoslava* of 1073 (Lotman, p. 87) seems pertinent here. It
speaks of a secret level of reading or a new step of textual
semantics: "There is something that has been said, but that
reason must understand otherwise."

Now, it is significant and theoretically important that in the
*Disputatio* it is precisely in an analytic study of the correlation of
levels of the text that an indication emerges of an ulterior symbolic level of reading or a semiological message of the text. It is
clear that in an allegorical text a relation of homomorphism or
isomorphism must exist between the manifest level and the
figured level—in our example, between the two different systems, the botanical and the ethical. For example, if the rose is

*olta in le rame / e bolda* (high on the branches / and self-assured), the qualification is clearly supposed to be referred to the rose and, at the same time, to pride. The same is true for the violet-humility, where the flower is born *aprova la terra* (close to the ground) or is placed *sot pei* (underfoot). If there is a gap in the isomorphic relation between the thematic and symbolic levels, we can say with the ancient Russian text that "here reason must understand differently," that is, understand the constructive principle that has led to the gap. Leaving aside this analysis of the break in the isomorphism between thematic and ethicosymbolic levels, I want for my purposes to refer to only one aspect of the problem: when a split exists between the first and the second, or symbolic, levels of reading, the isomorphism is reconstructed between the second and a third, or new, symbolic level which, in the example of this text, is sociopolitical, ideological. In this case, such an operation was suggested to the author because the predicates of the ethical level were subjects of that sociopolitical level—the *magnates* and the *cives*, respectively. Thus, in the *Disputatio* the ethicosymbolic level can be both: (a) the final arrival point for a more simple and general decoding, or a reading on the consumer level; and (b) a latch that links the thematic level to a third, sociopolitical level.

In the realization of this "semantic of many steps," the lexical level, the elements of which rest on more subtle semantic presuppositions, collaborates effectively. For example, syntagms like *officio de rapina* (act of violence) and *agnelli mansueti* (meek lambs), apparently innocuous, are in reality of a polysemic nature. The alert reader can decodify them inside the text's linguistic system, as precise allusions to the lexicon of the antimagnate statutes and see them as collaborating in the transmission of an ideological message. Naturally the structure of a trial with the lily as judge receives a different decoding at the third level, in that the accused are definite social groups.

To the readers of his time, Bonvesin offered a more simple or a more complex message, according to their capacity to decode. The different meanings do not annul each other but they are stratified and, with their coexistent presence, give rise to the highly ludic effect of art. What Lotman has to say about the author of the *Sermon* is valid generally: "It almost seems as if the author enjoys the abundance of senses and possible interpretations of the text. The mechanism of the ludic effect does not lie in the immobile, temporary coexistence of the meanings but in the constant consciousness of the possibility of other meanings" (see note 23).

We deduce from this that literary communication is attained rather differently on the synchronic, and above all on the diachronic, level. Synchronically, the macropolysemy of a text like the *Disputatio* provokes different grades of reading and comprehension; its own ambiguity favors the existential prudence of the author. On the diachronic plane, literary communication is made more difficult for decoders who are distant in time and outside the secondary referent of the text, the sociopolitical reality of its time; and this confirms the importance, for such decoders, of a sort of initiation to the text by way of an analytic and comparative inquiry, conducted on all levels of the text.

## 5. FORM OF THE CONTENT AND FORM OF THE EXPRESSION

One concept repeated from the time of the Russian Formalists until today is the need to relate each level of the text to one or more extratextual series, literary or not. I should refer to the already cited works of Pagnini, Segre, Beccaria; the last has recently investigated more deeply the question of horizontal confrontation between the meters of individual texts and the established metrical practice of the tradition.[24] As with a climbing plant, the roots are always elsewhere. For a consideration of the formal levels and their links with the various threads of literary language, registers and subcodes, see IIIa.4, while for the influence of the codification of literary genres on the bond between the thematic-symbolic, ideological, and formal levels in individual hypersigns, see Chapter V.

From the preceding considerations on the nature and function of textual levels and of critical praxis we can see that they tend to become polarized toward a "form of the content" and a "form of the expression." By the form of the content we mean the dynamic relation that is set up in a text between the contents, their unique organization, which is overdetermined symbolically and ideologically: in other words, the structural unity of the thematic, symbolic, and ideological levels. Lichačëv says that "the world of the literary work reproduces reality in a symbolic, 'abbreviated' variant"; in this world space, time, psychological conditions, the historical world, the moral world appear in a "total construction that is *proper* to the work, not to reality."[25] The work, that is, contracts, dilates, changes the perspectives, the relation of presences and absences. It is thus that the form of the content is born, giving new significance to the content.

The syntagm "form of the content" is adopted from Hjelmslev (as is "form of the expression"), but with a very different technical meaning in that it is used to deal with "form" not relatable to the code but to the message. Such terminological violence and extrapolation of a well-known model seems justified by the need to render the concept of a "formal," morphological organization of the content, on which the modelization takes place—and justified, too, because there does not exist in the language any synonym for "form" which is pertinent here.

The hypersign levels that have their origins in the forms (the phonic-timbric, morphosyntactic, rhythmic, at times the metric, the generically stylistic) meet in a higher transsentential unity. This unity results from the individual writer's struggle to shape a homogeneous language out of the heterogeneous one and his struggle with the second, or literary, language. This higher transsentential unity works as the large signifier of the text. The form of the content and the form of the expression interact to constitute the *invariant of the work*, which is more general and compact than are the single textual levels in their combinatorial game. That this is not a matter of terminological taste but of workable concepts is proven by a comparative study of several texts that belong to the same literary genre. The codification of a literary genre is a *program* constructed on very general laws that involve the relation between certain thematic-symbolic levels and certain formal levels; without such a relation codification does not exist. Inside every work the program of the genre becomes a constructive law of the work and gives rise to the form of the content and the form of the expression, which may be more or less innovative, more or less revolutionary (see chap. V). The generative structure of the work already carries with it an obligation that establishes a certain type of relation between the form of the content and the form of the expression. Whereas this obligation is at first conceived by the writer synthetically, the executed work will actualize it minutely through the interaction of all levels. For example, in a narrative text, to the form of the content belong both the plot and the organization of the psychological elements, while the *fabula* and the narrative model are the fruits of the logical operations of the critic analyzing the text.[26] To the form of the expression of the narrative text belongs the syntagmatic structure of the artistic language in which the action of the social-linguistic (language and literary language) has been subjected to an individual stylistic reelaboration and to the constructive law of the text. Therefore, if the analyst acts as a pure linguist, he will isolate linguistic classes or phenomena independently of the form of the expression and will refer, according to his aims, to historical or scientific categories of linguistic inquiry. The critic will emphasize instead the form of the expression, examining on the one hand the local, contextual, syntagmatic structure and on the other the transsentential unity of the whole text (IV.2, 3). In this case, the pure study of the linguistic microstructures obviously serves as a necessary presupposition. In the actual state of such studies it may be noted that suprasegmental research in Italy has made excellent contributions to the study of phonic-timbric and phonic-rhythmic elements, for example, in the work of Agosti and Beccaria. Further contributions may be expected in the systematic analyses of syntactic structures; for syntax, besides organizing what is enunciated on the page both connotatively and rhythmically, becomes a signifier or form of total relation, specific to the work, whose meaning coincides with the complex of relations that the writer has set up on the thematic-symbolic level (V.6).

The reciprocal relation ($\rightleftarrows$) between the form of the content and the form of the expression is basic to the scheme of literary communication proposed by Chatman,[27] even if he does not use our terminology. Chatman distinguishes in the narrative work the initial choice between mimetic and diegetic structure, between representation and story: "To specify the four possibilities that may result, I propose the following terms: 'to enact,' for enunciations of nonmediated or 'represented' processes; 'to recount,' for enunciations of 'recounted' actions; 'to present,' for enunciations of 'represented' stases; and 'to describe,' for enunciations of 'recounted' stases, remembering always that enunciated is used in an abstract sense, independent of all support." Now, whether a narrator or speaker is to be present or not involves a choice of form of the content, and the consequences of that choice are fundamental for the form of the expression as well as for the linguistic expression itself. Benveniste would say it is a question of the use of pronouns or of verbal forms when he distinguishes the level of *histoire* from that of *discours*.[28] In the acute examination by Chatman of several literary passages (Dostoevsky, Beckett, Capote), it turns out that the narrative discourse of itself so marks the formal level as to permit the author to express the modality of the action without the presence of any action verb unless that verb has meaning on the level of the story (Chatman, p. 16). But even more stimulating in Chatman's essay is the use of the theory of speech acts which are functions of both the form of the content and the form of the expression; the word acts of the narrator may not only be distinguished from those of the characters among themselves, but may produce a variety of effects, of "perlocutions," in their context, because they are surrounded by the ramifications of expressive particulars (see Chatman's comments about the opening sentences of *The Brothers Karamazov*). Thus the form of the content and the form of the expression work on the pragmatic level—on the way we receive the work—in that they are *other* with respect to the contents and language on which they are constructed. The historical-social position of the text is a result of this pragmatic action.

## 6. FUNCTIONALITY AND UNIQUENESS

It would be opportune now to connect this discussion of the hypersign with what has already been said in I.5 about the semiological typology of culture. The greater the writer the more likely he is to stand at the crossroads between the sociocultural sign system of his age and the indecipherability and profound ambiguity of the real. Precisely because he is in this position, no matter what theme he chooses, he manages to select elements with latent meaning, phenomena that are in themselves limited particulars, and to unite them in a way that expresses not a particular and limited message but a plurivalent one. A fragment of life thus transmits life, and therefore the possibility of a general ideological message (IIIb). This is the artistic principle by which the organization of something produces something else, something that is qualitatively different and therefore subject to many readings, decodifications, and destructuralizations, and capable in the end of renewing that very sociocultural semiotic system from which the author started.

Two concepts have developed in critical speculation about the artistic process that, it seems to me, require postscripts or rectification: the *functionality* and the *uniqueness* of the work of art.

The concept of functionality has been emphasized by structuralist critics who have studied the work as an object; the stronger and more profound the work—that is, more complex—the more its construction reveals a high grade of functionality. It is like saying that functionality is directly proportional to artistic realization. That is all very well as long as it is kept in mind that functionality is not a specific art principle; there are works realized according to all the rules of the functionality of levels that are nonetheless consumer products, and there are intellectual works—scientific demonstrations, for example—that function with an elegance that make them *seem* masterpieces. Functionality is not even the specific differentia of artistic perception on the part of the addressee.

As to the concept of uniqueness, the work of art is in effect a unique and unrepeatable organization; and one often lingers long over this concept. Valéry's famous remark, "Beautiful works are the daughters of their forms," becomes totally meaningful if it is used to refer to both the form of the content and the form of the expression, for it is from the reciprocal contact of these two forms that newness springs. That contact is both the internal *vis* and the equilibrium of every artistic organism. Uniqueness is the prerogative of the work considered as "closed." Despite the ambiguity of every poetic creation, classic works present an *apparent* naturalness that led Flaubert to write: "Masterpieces are beasts; they have the tranquil aspect of the productions of nature herself, of the large animals and of the mountains."[28a] This character of uniqueness and necessity gives the addressee the impression that things could not be otherwise, nothing more, nothing less; there already appears, in some sixteenth-century poetic theories, the concept of "essential form" as source of a *unicum*.[29] The movement of contemporary criticism is in two directions. On the one hand, it replaces the ontological and atemporal concept of the *unicum* with the historic-semiological concept. Uniqueness means either not being derived from the rules of the literary system and from the precise codifications of one of its laws or genres; or it may mean a different use of the rules themselves (for these two cases, cf.V.4). On the other hand, uniqueness resides in the unpredictability of the message in regard to the sociocultural series of the age as against the predictability of smoothly codified products. The concept of the "masterpiece" is due to a collective phenomenon of transformation: in the beginning there is a text; our use of it in time makes it, little by little, a masterpiece.

From the moment in which the different readings by addressees start the process of use (IIb), the work, according to Eco, may be defined as "open."[30] But a more specific determination of the open work exists in this contemporary period, and with a different typology. These typologies range from *the work in movement*, or unfinished work, on which the user collaborates, to the message that Eco (1962, p. 84) calls *plurivocal*, to certain very recent experiments in poetic and prose texts that pile up several lyric or narrative arguments one on the other in an attempt to reproduce the stratified character of the unconscious and conscious stages of the narrating I, the dissemination of sense through the page. These are texts that seek to escape from structure but in reality give us fugal structures. If writing is "a way of forming," in effect the "formed" *is*, it happens in the precise way in which it happens, it obeys its constructive law. In other words, the problem of "opening" as a nonstructurable phase pertains to the sender and the addressee, not to the text in itself, no matter how plurivalent it may be. There is the danger today that some writers are excessively influenced by the "ruling class" of literary theorists and transform creation into artistic paraphrases of artistic theory. In that case, for the good of poetry we perhaps should hope that the ruling class of theorists brings its historic mission quickly to a close.

## 7. MACROTEXT

To the concept of the text as hypersign, as a complex of verbal signs that represent, as Eco says, the *"status of a supersign-function,"*[31] it is fruitful to add the concept of a semiotic unity that stands above the text—what we call the *macrotext*.

This concept is applicable, in determined conditions only, to a group of poetic or prose texts by the same author; in other words, a collection of poems or stories may be simply a group of texts gathered together for diverse reasons, or that collection may be in itself the configuration of a large unitary text, or macrotext. In this second case, every single poetic or prose text is a microstructure that is articulated inside a macrostructure, hence the functional and informative character of the collection. It is like saying that the total meaning does not coincide with the sum of the partial meanings of single texts, but goes beyond it. Going back to the first, and more common, case, when a writer gathers together for the addressees a certain number of writings that are coherent enough and therefore subject to grouping, the definition of a collection as a group of texts is only a tautology.

The functionality and information possibility of a collection as such occurs when at least one of the following conditions is present: (1) if there exists a combination of thematic and/or formal elements that runs through all the texts and produces the unity of the collection; (2) if there is a progression to the discourse for which each single text can occupy only one place. Clearly, the second condition presupposes the first, but the reverse is not true.

As examples, we turn to two recent works, one a collection of poems, the other of stories. M. Santagata, in an article, "Intertextual Connections in the *Canzoniere* of Petrarch,"[32] studies the connections of transformation from one text to another and the connections of equivalence (parallel repetition of similar elements, etc.), individuates and distinguishes the superficial structural elements from the "deep structural elements hypothesized under the form of a thematic paradigm," and concludes that the *Canzoniere* meets the conditions of both (1) and (2) of our scheme.

In an article, "Text or Macrotext? The Stories of Marcovaldo by Italo Calvino,"[33] I myself have applied this type of inquiry to the two series of tales that have Marcovaldo as protagonist, the first from 1958 (ten stories) and the second from 1963 (the same ten stories plus ten new ones). The first group turns out to be a macrotext, the second, not. In addition, in the first the repetitive succession of fundamental actions allows for the extrapolation of a model or generative structure of the ten texts. This model, on the one hand, helps to realize the intertextual links on the level of the handling of the *fabula,* and on the other, it serves as the connection between the deep ideological motivation—underneath all the stories—and the single imaginative creations. The collection, homogenous and organic, turns out to be a macrotext according to the criteria of (1) and (2), while this is not the case in the second series of twenty tales, which contains, however, several among the finest stories dedicated to Marcovaldo. This means that the critic must follow another route to interpret them, keeping in mind the diachronic process and the consequent transformation of the ideological motivation and the formal level.

## 8. THE SYSTEM OF COMMUNICATION OF THE WRITER

The case of the second collection of Calvino's stories leads to the question of the placement of an artistic hypersign in a writer's total production. We may proceed in either of two directions: to an examination of the semiotic system or total communicative reality of a writer in function of the single text or of the structure of the text in function of the system.

In the first case, we should study the invariants of the system in order to individuate their presence in the single text: key words of symbolic value that point to the extratext, stylistic connotators, reused material.[34] Such an approach gives a monocentric perspective, the meaning and communicative system of an author in function of one of his texts.

The perspective becomes polycentric when the single texts are seen as stages of a journey, structures of transformation of a system, moments in the continuity or discontinuity of a productive I from the early to the late works. Gottfried Benn has written knowingly on the double process which the creative phases of a writer undergo: for some, a precocious maturity and late uncertainty, for others the reverse, that is, the greatest potential arrived when the end is near.[35] Therefore, except in exceptional cases, the artist's development is not a foregone conclusion, nor does each phase imply the next. The artist's motivations that produce the transformation of the system of meaning and communication are tied on one side to the internal journey of the productive I,[36] and on another to the extratextual influences, the sociocultural and historical conditions, the ideological pressures of certain aspects of the real. An artist's development in his journey is, in a certain way, the representation through his various works of this double thrust. To unite the several texts of a writer is essentially to unite the supersign-functions of each of them. While we may find a greater or lesser grade of stability—or almost none at all—it is nevertheless difficult indeed for the critic to master the chain reactions.

# V. Literary Genres and Codifications

## 1. POSSIBLE DEFINITIONS: LITERARY GENRES AND SOCIAL STRATA

Save in exceptional cases, the text does not live isolated in literature; because of its sign function, it belongs with other signs to a group, to a literary genre. Genre serves as the place where the individual work enters into a complex network of relations with other works. But such a general definition is not, as Aristotle would say—along with his sixteenth-century exegetes, the authors of poetics—"speech that shows us the essence of the thing."[1] In fact, if one starts from such a definition, inquiries into literary genres lead to very distinct conclusions that may be separated into two fundamental categories: those of an abstract, atemporal, deductive nature and those of a historic, diachronic, inductive nature.[2]

The first category is subject to further subdivision, for the abstract, deductive inquiry can start from general structures that are anthropological or—instead—rhetorical. In the first approach, which has flourished in contemporary poetics, a reflection on anthropological structures (for example, on the fantastic) leads to the discovery of fundamental properties from which the genre is deduced—lyric, dramatic, epic, fantastic, etc.—and, consequently, to the typology of literary "dis-

115

course," or better, of literary types that correspond to anthropological structures. In effect, the theory of genres becomes the theory of literary discourse, which we then seek to
formalize; theory thus concerns not only works already written
but those that are possible and not yet written—theory is directed toward a principle of the generation of *types* of texts.[3] In
the second approach, followed in Classical and Renaissance
poetics, it is basic rhetorical structures that are responsible for
conferring a normative character to genre theory: literary genre
is the place of encounter for certain thematic and formal
possibilities, for certain models, for which examples are offered
by Aristotle's *Poetics* and the Italian poetics of the sixteenth
century. The latter elaborate on Aristotle's principles of imitation, and on the *Ars Poetica* of Horace coupled with the rhetoric
of Cicero or under the influence of medieval rhetoric; and in
this environment a hierarchy of values or a pyramidal order of
genres is constructed.[4] As Genot has already shown, the principle of imitation of this kind of poetic is the result of an act in
which "the historic, generative, and relatively psychological
notion of the *archetype*" is transformed into the notion of a
practical normative model.[5] This normative notion of the
theory of genres extends and works through a long time
period, from Hellenism to the end of the eighteenth century.[6]
This is followed by an evolutionary theory, elaborated by
Brunetière and Symonds—and modern epigones are not lacking.[7] Unfortunately, evolutionary theories are tied more to the
standard concepts of Darwin amidst which they arose than to
the reality of literary genres; for the innovating products of
literature usually arise for reasons contrary to evolution, that is,
from deviations from the specific codifications of a genre, as
well as through spontaneous individual impulses.

These approaches are opposed by the historical-inductive
approach, complemented and corroborated by structuralist
methods (the latter make possible synchronic cuts in the diachronic development of genres and allow for confrontations
that tend to shed light on the dynamics of history). Such an

approach makes use of two facts of primary importance. In the first place, it poses the problem of the transformation of literary genres and of their functions, a phenomenon that can be explained only by reference to a temporal and historic dimension. These latter dimensions must also be used to explain the presence of different genres in various eras or the contamination by one genre of another, whereas deductive theories can only refer to a literary reality constructed in watertight compartments. In addition, a historic-diachronic perspective relates genres to the universe of senders and addressees, and can contribute to our understanding of literary communication and of the relations between literature and society.

If Lotman's contention is true, and "the genre may appear as a unique text, but it is impossible to make of it the object of an artistic perception,"[8] it is also true that the choice of a genre on the part of the writer implies his choice of a certain interpretive model of reality, either on the thematic or formal levels. Every genre carries its own restrictions on what can be gathered from the real or the verisimilar; it has a selective and provocative function, its codes are never neutral but are—so to speak—like human inventions of long duration that direct the message, in its role as message, in a certain direction.

We can thus speak of authorial competence: the writer chooses a literary genre and, accepting the rules of the game that are already known to him, he finds it economical to channel his own creative forces within that genre. In other words, the literary genre offers an initial physiognomy and conditions the sign quality of the characters, the themes, the motifs; it leaves its mark on the signifiers, on the structure that these assume, and on their contextual use. Naturally, periods and genres of strong norms and codifications (the adjective "strong" is Umberto Eco's) alternate with those of weak norms and codifications that are more subject, by their nature, to violations.

The literary genre is, however, also a *symptom* of a culture and of the social group that produces, receives, and distributes it; hence, the importance of considering the notion of the competence of the addressees, a consideration undervalued up to now in histories of literature. The very question of the relation between literature and society (see I.4) would yield more fruitful answers if sociological critics were to focus not only on single texts, even if by the greater writers, but on the articulation of literary genres. Because of their "reality" and because even minor writers make use of them, genres are more linked to the sociocultural context and its stratifications than are single works. It is not an easy question to deal with because literary genres have, in their history, something in common with language. They last longer than the sociocultural reasons that created them, so that—like language itself—they are often slower moving than the advance of society—apart from their possible existence as fossils. This said, it is nevertheless true that every genre seems to be directed toward a certain type of public, sometimes even to a specific class, whose expectations are directed toward that genre as long as social conditions warrant. The phenomenon is well summarized by Koehler:

> When, because of modifications in the infrastructure, the internal contradictions of the society have become so acute that the literary superstructure is not capable of containing them, the old quantities are brusquely transformed into new qualities, that is to say that new forms and new themes supplant the old ones. This does not at all mean the rejection of the entire tradition. It is conserved to the extent that it is able to serve as a means of expression for the new content. Motifs and literary genres remain alive as long as they are able to cover a function inside the new poetic world or, in other terms, as long as they are able to serve as the esthetic mediation between being and consciousness.[9]

A striking example, cited by Koehler, is the French prose romance of the thirteenth century. Because the rise of the monarchy had by now frustrated the aspirations of the lower nobility (knights-errant) to integrate itself through great adventures into the high nobility and had produced a radical transformation in social relations, the new romance in prose preserved the adventure of the courtly romance as a structural element but changed its function; it made that adventure the instrument of a religious *quête* (the Grail) or of forms suggestive of self-destruction. An analogous analysis could be made of the amorous symbolism in the Duecento lyric with its passage from the feudal celebration of *nobilitas generis* to that of *nobilitas animi*, a concept born in the new context of the bourgeoisie.[10] The phenomenon becomes more apparent in genres of large social consumption: the picaresque novel changes the hero of the chivalric romance into an antihero—a sign of altered times—or handles him in vigorously comic fashion. Through succesive changes of function, from the picaresque novel the modern novel is born, as we well know.[11] A contemporary example of the rules of a genre working toward a new result is to be found in the Proppian fairy tale of the ideologized theatre of Antonio Porta: *La presa di potere di Ivan lo Sciocco* (The Seizure of Power by Ivan the Stupid).

The problem of literary genres in the perspective here expounded is therefore ambivalent; on the one hand it involves the functional variations inside the literary system and in relation to that system—a problem studied first by Shklovsky and Tynjanov; on the other, the problem becomes the special one of literary communication that involves senders and addressees and sheds new light on the history of the reception of texts in varied sociocultural contexts and movements.[12]

## 2. CONDITIONS OF CODIFICATION

As we noted at the beginning of this chapter, a literary genre may be defined as the place where the individual work enters into a complex network of relations with other works. From such a vantage what is pertinent is the nature of the relations that are set up and their character as invariants, so that, in a certain sense, genre can be called a type of literary process. In this regard it is worth noting that, on a thematic level, what is significant in a genre is not so much the presence of any content, theme, or motif which may be common to several literary genres (for example, the themes of love, seduction, treachery, war, etc.) but rather the relation between the thematic organization and the formal level, without which there is no genre. Themes and motifs in themselves are like the timber in Trissino's lovely simile, which we would dare to make ours by transferring it into another context: "Of a quantity of timber, worked in a certain way and assembled in a certain manner, one makes a galley, but of other timber, and in another manner, one makes a caravel; and of still other, a brigantine; and these forms depend on the quantity, quality, and assemblage of the said timber, but are something different from it."[13] Similes aside, in a genre the theme is so strictly tied to the formal level that *only from interdependence does codification arise.* Besides this, we could hardly speak of codes if there were no rules of interaction between the form of the content and the form of the expression.[14] Therefore, if we limit ourselves to agreeing with Todorov[15] that the genre is the coagulation of certain thematic and formal possibilities common to a series of works, there still remains unexplored the problem of the way in which, from the relations set up among various works, codification takes place. Actually the Russian Formalists had already maintained the importance of the principle of correspondence between the creation or mutation of thematic material and the creation or mutation of forms. From this, we can very simply deduce the link—in any case, obvious—between structures of contents and structures of forms. But if our inquiry is conducted concretely on a more or less homogeneous corpus of texts, which is what a compact literary genre is, it can proceed to an examination of the invariants that give life to the code (as distinct from the variants of the individual texts) and of the rules of transformation of the codes themselves.

To sketch in now what will soon become clear in detail, here are some possible operations of an inductive nature in relation to a literary genre:

(a) Extracting from a comparison of the structure of works an analysis of the invariants, the principles that generate and regulate codification.

(b) Investigating the rules of transformation of a genre on a spatial and, above all, a temporal level; among the works ascribed to a genre a chain of continuity is created, and across the distance of many of its rings, a change takes place on the axis of codification. Sometimes the transformation is realized traumatically, or though the intervention of a highly innovative personality (see IV.1), or for specific motivations that belong to the entire literary system (the Baroque, Romanticism, etc.).

(c) Analyzing the process of restoration of a genre after a long period in which the place of that genre in the system had been unoccupied, a null position. In such cases restoration may involve the recuperation of a genre that functioned in other eras inside the literary system of that same national literature (for example, the current mode of the Mannerist treatise of seventeenth-century provenance), or of a genre that lived in the system of another literature (for example, the Italian classic theatre in the sixteenth century). In either case, the insertion will provoke shifts within the system.

(d) Extracting models—once it has been made clear how the codification functions—through a process of "reduction"; that is, bringing formalization to bear on a corpus that is obviously homogeneous. At this point formalization can be productive insofar as it acts on a series of texts and can derive very general and conventionalized elements.

## 3. LITERARY GENRE AS PROGRAM

Within every genre, it is obvious that codification does not have those normative characteristics that it would have in a linguistic or legal system, but rather it has a program constructed on very general laws. These laws pertain to the dynamic relation between certain thematic-symbolic levels and certain formal levels of the genre, and the whole stands in a distinctive or oppositional relation to the program of another genre.[16] In addition, we must consider the existence of sub-genres which have traits of the genre as well as their own differentiated traits: processes of affiliation with homogeneous development. Within each member work of a genre, the program becomes embodied in constitutive laws of the work itself insofar as it is a closed reality. The constitutive law or general structure of a text is perceived as such precisely because it does not coincide fully with the program—it is more complex and dynamic. For example, the stylistic choices inside a single work, on the one hand, are correlated on the stylistic level up to a point consonant with the specific form and, on the other, they are conditioned by the corresponding choices that the writer has made on the other planes or levels of the work (IV.2, 3).

The nature of the program implicit in the codification of a genre belongs to the competence of the senders, who individuate in the genre not only the place of works already written, but also of the works they may write; it is the place of expectation, the road that awaits their journey. In periods like ours, periods of crisis in the literary system, the roads of the genres seem closed to creative traffic, and the program seems to function only if lowered to the level of mass communication: popular novels, detective stories, historical or other novels written for television, stories in popular magazines, advertising messages, etc.—all texts in which there is almost no deviation between code and message. That is, in praxis a clear distinction of a social nature is created with reference to different strata of the public or to different pragmatic moments of the decoding (i.e., airplane literature or literature for traveling and relaxation). At a higher level, the ideological, extraliterary crisis, which calls into question the very concept of literature as a system, is felt by the more aware writers; and this crisis has coincided with the contemporary loss of the esthetic function of genres. We have, then, a negative proof of the importance of codification in a genre; the writer, feeling estranged from the objects of the tradition, violates their laws of construction, and returns, for example, to certain formal levels (the current renewal of metric structures of the past and also of rhyme) or to thematic levels that he deliberately deforms (viz., the chivalric tradition in the works of Italo Calvino). The genres are in crisis because the codifications that regulated the thematic-formal relation are broken. The result is that motifs, stylemes, formal structures move today like the wreckage of a sunken ship; they land wherever a wave sends them, off the course that was imposed by their specific codes. Antonio Porta, a poet of the avant-garde who is now in search of a new way, writes: "The current of poetry-making follows impossible roads, it advances into paths deemed at first sight impractical, and while it ceases to flow, it is blocked, frozen, in the face of the officialness, of the bombast, of the impositions of an indiscriminate, obtuse, cultural establishment."[17] Naturally one must not confuse the relation between the entire literary system of an era and its socioideological system—a relation that is theoretically and historically controllable in its several dimensions—with relations between the single literary genre and ideology—relations that are rather less binding or definable; it is even true that a controversial literary work can be fashioned through the use of an old genre (V.6). In other words, the genre in itself can be a neutral institution that only assumes ideological content through its relations with other institutions of the literary system.

Still at a general level, it may be observed that in eras when the genres have vitality, the writer not only is competent in the program of the literary genre to which he adheres: he also draws on the entire performance-system of the literary language (IIIa.1, 3). In fact, even though it can be shown that every genre has had its own type of formal organization—whether it was imposed on a monolinguistic or a plurilinguistic basis—every writer has nevertheless come to terms with the general rhetorical structures of the literary language; above all, literary language in a country like Italy has been the substitute for the nonexistent *langue* (IIIa.4). This particular historic situation of the Italian language, that is, the lack of a national language of communication that acts on the literary language, has resulted in the latter being much more static, at least in the past, with respect to the other levels of the literary system. The constant presence through the centuries of many markers of rhetorical origin on the formal level of almost every Italian genre, the presence, that is, of a so-called "transgeneric" source, gives the curious impression in Italian literature that something is always different, but something is always the same.

Still very important in the general perspective of the literary system as an interaction of genres and their codification is the existence of another collecting channel, that of dialect, of language facts used mainly for expressionistic purposes. Dialect, in contrast to the common rhetorical structures, flowers only in certain literary genres and not in others, and more in certain eras than in others—and most obviously when dialect detaches itself from language. The insertion of regional subcodes occurs where the specific program of certain literary genres permits it, and produces a type of relation with the thematic level that is codified in each of these genres. For example, dialect in the rustic-*nenciale* genre [from Nencia, the Tuscan name often used for the female present in this genre—A.M.] has a function very different from its function in sixteenth-century comedy, even if the writers of both use dialect for expressionist purposes.

## 4. PRINCIPLES OF THE CODIFICATION OF A GENRE

Whatever literary moment we take into consideration, we find literary genres in which stable, conventional links already exist. These links do not joint together contents but, rather, a certain mode of treating determined contents (for example, love in the *Stilnovo* and love in Petrarchism) and the *already oriented* formal resolution of these contents. They are almost models to which the collectivity of producers and consumers is accustomed, models validated through constant use. When the artistic message is seen in relation to literary codes, a process is begun that may be summarized as follows: on the one hand, there are the codifications that by themselves tend to be canonized; on the other, there are the messages of single writers that can act in two directions—either to transform the codes from the inside or to corrode and subvert them to the point of destroying them. The correlation of messages and codes is a profitable critical-semiological operation because the insertion of the single text or hypersign in its rightful place in the evolution of a genre clarifies its individual qualities, its dosages of originality and convention; at the same time it also sheds light on the process of literary communication through the evolution of contents and of forms both in themselves and in relation to historic-social contexts.

Here is the place to expand on points (a) and (b) schematized above (V.2). We shall take two genres as exemplary because they have the advantage of being similar in their themes, yet very clearly characterized and "typified," at least in the second half of the fifteenth century: the bucolic genre that we shall call B and the rustic-*nenciale* that we shall call R. Varchi in his *Ercolano* had already theorized two possibilities or modes in which "to sing pastoral things," "one in jest and the other true," to use his own words. They are also two different condensations of thematic material.

The two chosen genres, having in common their pastoral-rustic themes, allow a distinct individuation of the ensemble of elements common to B and R, that is the intersection of B and R, and the unshared elements, that is the disjunction of B and R. The intersection may be represented graphically, for clarity, by using Venn diagrams:

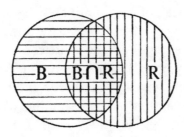

The zones comprising only B and only R are those in which the specific codifications of the two genres take place. Naturally in both B and R the theme contains constants or invariants, typical of that given genre, and variants ascribable to single texts; here it is the invariants that are of interest. In B they are reused materials inherited from classical bucolic poetry—but it is the new form of the content that avoids their automatization:[18] (1) the place of the events, Arcadia or pseudo-Arcadia, with the special characteristics of an idyllic land; (2) the copresence of divinities (rivers made divine, nymphs, etc.), of shepherds and shepherdesses, besides historic personages represented as shepherds; (3) the author of the text himself figures as a shepherd, with the consequent mixing of two narrative "aspects" (author $\rightleftarrows$ character); (4) in the dialogic eclogue, disputes or contrasts or debates predominate, with two or three shepherds serving alternately as senders or addressees; frequently there are alternating songs with amorous content, and these can be structured in a narrative sequence. These four elements, insofar as they are bucolic materials, have an auxiliary function, while the primary function is a result of the new form of the content and produces a relative homogeneity in the fifteenth-century corpus. That is, the idyllic locus, the shepherds, and their *tenzoni* (contests) become, in the organization of the contexts, vehicles of an allegorical meaning (through the development of fourteenth-century premises— though in the fourteenth century the symbolic material served for didactic ends). They represent the Humanist environment and its protagonists, often identifiable behind the recurring pastoral names. Across everything, what the poets of B call the "pastoral veil" is extended. The shift comes about by a leap across "fields of images,"[19] since there is no contiguity on the conceptual level between the shepherds and the Humanists. At this point, a comparative analysis of the plots of the single eclogues studied by segmenting their themes shows that the texts, on the level of the form of the content, are put together through a binary process of isomorphism: every narrative sequence is both itself and figurative—it belongs to both the objective and subjective planes. The classification, which will be discussed elsewhere, shows how the functions of the bucolic actors not only change but grow. For example, the motif of the assault on the sheep by the wolves turns from a description into a plot element; it takes on a function inside the symbolic context in that wolves are the equivalents of enemies on the literary or political level, the adversaries of the Humanist shepherds. There is also a change in function in the amoebaean [alternately answering, responsive] song, which now serves as the carrier of a specific discourse. The structural, morphological change of function in one of the constitutive levels of the genre—the thematic—produces that radical transformation, and consequently what were the secondary traits of the classical genre become fundamental in fifteenth-century poetry.

In B, to the new form of the content, there corresponds on the formal level an organic operation that involves, correlationally, both the metrical and lexical levels: an exceptional polymetrics, organized within the closed form of the eclogue, and the creation of a series of *sdrucciole* rhymes [accented on the antepenultimate], that is, of families of rhyme words that bounce from one text to another. On the level of expression, the opposition between the pastoral world and the Humanist symbolism produces a state of coexistence-opposition between refined Latinisms and rustic words. That is, two lexical series that normally lead to mutual exclusions in the literary language, because they are typical of two different linguistic codes, here coexist and connote each other in turn in a new way. Because it is systematic, this oppositional connotation illuminates the process by which the bucolic norm takes off at the meeting place between the form of the content and the form of the expression. In addition, the plurilingualism often results in the rhetorical figure of *obscuritas* (the eclogues of Arsocchi are typical) with the aim of complicating on the thematic level the relation between the two "fields of images."

We come now to R, the rustic-*nenciale* genre. Here, on the thematic level, the number of narrative functions and actors is minimal with respect to B. The characters who polarize the functions, that is, the *actants*, are two: the amorous couple, the shepherdess-peasant with fixed names (in Tuscany Nencia, Tonia, Beca, Nanna, etc.; in the North Zoanina, Togna), the addressee of the love song, and the shepherd-peasant who tries to win her with song (we are in an agricultural culture in which the shepherd is also a peasant). R is therefore a more compact genre with minimal thematic variations, and can be easily formalized.[20] The fact that the narrative functions are reduced to a minimum leads to this first consequence: while in B every eclogue is a closed text in which narrative sequences are distributed, in R the composition is potentially open and, in the texts most faithful to the genre, constructed with a pure succession of octaves (*rispetti* or *strambotti*) whose end is not justified by reasons of the plot.[21]

The invariants of R are the following: (1) the place, which is no longer of an Arcadian type, but an anti-city (country or hills); (2) the rustic love song that consists of fixed motifs, among which predominate (a) the shepherd's boast, (b) the burst of rage with invective, (c) the offer of gifts, (d) a series of biting comparisons taken from rustic life to comment on feminine beauty, (e) an equivocal use, with sexual implications, of pastoral and agricultural terminology, (f) the display of visceral organs bursting from the anguish of love.[22]

In B the antecedent of the genre was classic bucolic poetry subject to transformations of a symbolic type in which the secondary traits of the genre have become primary. In R, the antecedent is the *pastorella* ("shepherdess") genre with parodic transformations in which the caricature of the seduction has become the primary trait. Thus, the love song in R is the opposite of the pastoral love song in B: the woman is not an object of communication but of a game.

The codification of R is also set in motion at the meeting place between the new thematic and formal levels, and a situation results that is particularly interesting from the point of view of theory: there is a binary movement, organically structured, on the stylistic level and on the strictly linguistic level. On the stylistic level there are fixed stylemes of a rustic origin symmetrical with those of the aulic love song and therefore blatantly parodic (for example, the tastiness of the woman compared to that of cheese). These stylemes have an interregional life in Tuscan, Bergamasque, or old Paduan texts. On strictly linguistic levels, especially phonetic and morphosyntactic, regional and even municipal subcodes are produced, and in these subcodes there is a systematic emergence of forms drawn from the separate Italian dialects, used consciously and expressionistically. The theoretical interest derives from the fact that in the codification of R, the ideological-thematic level, here the parody of the rustic world, is directly correlated to the rhetorical-stylistic level, while the level of language presupposes a choice among various regional and municipal subcodes—a deliberate choice if we find Bolognese authors who compose rustic texts in the old dialect of Padua, or Veronese authors who compose in Bergamasque. We thus have a double formal statute, accepted coherently by those faithful to the genre; and then the texts, inserted in a series, have a general signifier to which may converge a certain number of variable dialects, permissible in the genre.

As we have seen in the diagram, R and B contain a zone of intersection owing to the presence of common motifs and thematic traits. The existence of a zone of intersection between two contiguous genres in the literary system is important because it can be the origin of the future transformation of one of the two into the function of the other.

In the beginning the motifs common to B and R are constant but not essential; they belong to the background and margins of the thematic-material descriptions of the seasons or of rustic work, the release of beasts to pasture, the momentary loss of an animal from sight, the return to the hut at sunset, etc. At a certain moment in the history of R the corpus ceases to be homogeneous; one of the *nenciale* texts recently discovered by Domenico De Robertis[23] reveals how, through the influence of B, there enters into R the theme of the contest between two shepherds, one of whom recounts to the other—though with rustic traits—his encounter with the shepherdess and his falling in love. The event announces the entrance of a bucolic situation typical of B into R: a character who functions as narrator and a narrative sequence. This fact is interesting in regard to the problem of codification; these hybrid rustic texts avoid the open form of the octave in favor of the more closed form of the ballad and above all show an enormous reduction or even disappearance of all vernacular subcodes and expressionistic use of rustic language that had been formal qualities of R. In other words, an actor and a narrative sequence of B, now passed into R, has caused an explosion in the codification of the genre on all levels. Naturally, this occurs when the invariants of a genre—that is, the constructive elements of one genre, transferred to another—are the dominant elements. A comparative structural study of genres inside the literary system shows that often a genre, when it becomes a hybrid like R in the rustic texts of the type discovered by De Robertis (that is, no longer possessing efficient codification), tends to be transformed quickly into something else, starts a new process of thematic and formal organization that leads to models of a new codification. In our example, the dialogue of the shepherds inserted in the R context prepares for the birth, in the beginning of the sixteenth century, of the new genre of rustic theatre. The variability of a hybrid genre is a negative confirmation of the structural value of the codification.

The theoretical implications of the movement of the hybrid work just described are many. We can see the following: (1) the chain of contiguity, through which the codifying axis, across the distance of several links, may shift; (2) given number 1, the emergence of new models of codification may occur through the work of minor writers or so-called "obscure poets." This means that while, on the one hand, the texts of minor writers, constituting the connective tissue of literature, produce stability and, at the limit, the force of inertia, on the other hand, if these texts are subjected to a serial, relational scrutiny and a possibly fruitful, statistical scrutiny, they then testify to the slow, progressive movement of some codified traits and the regressive movement of others up to the point where the basic codification enters into crisis.

Returning to a comparison of R and B, we find that the corpus of R allows a study of the transformation and final crisis of a genre without the occurrence of the macroscopic and violent phenomenon that is the entrance upon the scene of a great actor, who, whether he modifies the codification from the inside of the genre or whether he breaks it, is always an element of sudden innovation which upsets the tendency toward stability in the system. In B, instead, there enters Jacobo Sannazaro, the author of *Arcadia*. It is an instructive example of how a great work throws program and models into crisis. Sannazaro revolutionizes the genre by degrees. The process, schematically represented, is as follows: (1) side by side with the eclogue are prose passages that already deviate structurally from the bucolic code: in that code, the presentation of the shepherds and of the reasons for their dialogue took place in the eclogue itself and were juxtaposed with the song; in Sannazaro, they take on the relation of the frame to the framed; (2) starting with Prose VI there is an increase in narrative sequences with new features: (a) the dominant role of the shepherd who says "I"; (b) a chain reaction that sets up a complex relationship among the various shepherds and the character who says "I," by which the bucolic shifts from static to dynamic. Actually, with the *Arcadia*, a new genre, the pastoral romance, is born.

To conclude, the rustic theatre and the pastoral romance *Arcadia* are stimulating examples of the two antithetical processes by which the codifications of R and B underwent a critical change.

## 5. PROCESSES OF TRANSFORMATION: THE FUNCTION OF MINOR AND MAJOR WRITERS

As we have seen, the rules of the genre fix the roles of the constituent parts. Still another example is the relation between semantic and metric traits in the sonnet and the canzone inside the Petrarchan genre, of such efficiency and durability in the Italian literary system—and not only the Italian. Here standard products and those of an artistic level coexist with differing functions. That is, minor authors tend to guarantee the constant validity and stability of the genre, which is why the process of transformation is so slow that it can be noticed only across the distance of many links in the chain. For us today it may require a certain effort to understand the power that the canonization of a genre has exercised over its duration. Certain literary traditions, like ethicoreligious traditions, are breathed in with the air itself, and just as no one living reflects on the existence of air but merely breathes it, so many minor writers have breathed, especially in the second half of the fifteenth century, the Petrarchism of their age. This is only natural, even though from a distance it may appear strange and wearying, because from a distance the temptation arises to decodify sonnets and canzone in the light of codes different from those common to both senders and addressees of an era. It is like saying that from a distance the great writers are not only enjoyed more but understood better than the minor writers; the offense to the norm is more enjoyable than obsequiousness to it. So that, unless philology and sociological and semiological criticism do not revive interest in them, there is a fatal absence of *pietas* toward minor writers, who are actually the connective tissue of literary institutions, the protagonists of their stability. Let it be understood, however, that a healthy *distinguo* must always be made between minor and minor: some minor writers contain surprises in reserve—and often they are the least known writers—writers capable of suddenly attaining very high levels, so that only an acute critic is capable of noticing them or is inclined to construct subgroups with a precise but not obvious physiognomy. (One example: the Petrarchists of the Po Valley, who are still to be recognized as such in critical appraisal.) The process of conservation and oblivion, in effect the process of communication, is complicated. It may well happen that the force of stability and the literary conventions of an era have banished just that handful of minor writers who are in their way artistically heretical, who disturbed the taste of the addressees, their habits of decodification, and that the effects of that banishment have continued to our day.

If we focus on literary genres as social phenomena of artistic communication, then we come to assign value to the function of minor writers, counterbalancing that thrust of history which, as Corneille said, scorns the leaving of signs of human struggle, unless those struggles have touched important men. Besides, in the specific Italian context with its regional cultures, attention to genres and subgenres in their ramifications (similar to what art history has been doing for so long) allows us to focus on centers of diffusion and of innovation in literary processes beyond a fictive panorama of unity.

As for the major writers, they displace the axis of codification according to a process that has been clearly illustrated by Mukařovský: "The living work of art always oscillates between the past and the future state of the norm: the present is best understood as a tension between the past norm and its violation, destined to become part of the future norm."[24] In other words, the process of transformation inside a literary genre does not become critical until the very existence of its codification is called into question, but it only partly modifies it. It is like saying that *the transformation also has regulative power.* In every hypersign of strong individuality the program of the literary genre matures and is modified as it becomes a constitutive law of the work itself. Successively, as was well noted by Mukařovský, the structure of this work "can be broken down into single particular norms that may now, without damage, be applied even outside the structure in which they originated." From the moment in which such a process takes place, the transformation, which was an individual event, becomes another link in the chain that is the path of a literary genre. Naturally, not all the aspects of a genre experience this transformation with equal liveliness.

A genre may be transformed by itself from the inside by a change in the function of one of its constitutive elements, following which the traits that are secondary in one era become primary in another; the genre reproduces like a microsystem those functional variations that generate the very movement of literature. Apropos of this, Shklovsky has spoken acutely of the heredity that passes from uncle to nephew giving privilege to and canonizing the younger branches of the family. An example has been given in V.4 apropos of bucolic materials and their functional change from the Classical to the Renaissance eras.

In addition, a genre is also transformed by changes in the other genres in the literary system, which means that there cannot be a history of a genre in isolation; on the contrary, every phenomenon of correlation and influence must be considered. If it is true, for example, that a good number of Italian literary genres have a percentage of themes and stylemes of Petrarchan origin, it is also true that a serial and diachronic study—perhaps by statistical methods—of Petrarchan texts would reveal an inverse process. It is not only the genres that change but their own hierarchy, which is differently constituted from one era to another; and this has consequences in the diachronic process of the various literary institutions, because in a certain sense, internal variations of opposing phenomena are taking place.

There is, in addition, a third type of displacement in the literary system, both more subtle and considerable. When large artistic and cultural developments take place—for example, that of the Baroque or of Romanticism—a kind of density is produced in the literature that renders it more homogeneous, as if it were nourished equally in all its parts. In such cases, the literary genres, while preserving their autonomous structures, are displaced coaxially in a certain direction, as if a unifying spiritual principle had intervened. This phenomenon touches both codes and individual messages; at the beginning of his brilliant and original essay on Racine, Giraudoux invites us to meditate on the fact that in solar ages like that of Pericles or of Louis XIV, there exists a finished culture in which an individual genius cannot gain much ground in the face of the talent of the society as a whole, as if to say that that very culture has become genius. In such periods the network of the general, interartistic invariants is strengthened—for example, the invariants that are used to decode a Baroque painting or a Baroque statue or a text in Baroque prose—and this leads to a deepening of the idea of cultural typology and, thus, of artistic communication related to a period as a whole. Models common to verbal and nonverbal texts, that is to different sign systems, can be found in the single levels of artistic hypersigns as well as in their way of interacting. The work on Mannerism and the Baroque by Ezio Raimondi, Mario Praz, Jean Rousset, and Jacqueline Risset, all of a high critical quality, has deepened our understanding of the levels of motifs, of tropes, and of symbols. For example, in regard to Petrarchism, Risset has called attention to the motif of tears, which from a "symbol of immobile, meditative suffering" of Petrarchan origin has become in Baroque Petrarchism a water motif, an image of liquidness and transparency (sea, river, lymph) in a manner such that "from the register of pain 'one slides' to that of spectacle," of theatrical visuality.[25] Analogously, Pozzi has followed the structural transformations of the trope of the rose.[26] Starting from an examination of the "thematic and figural seminary" rather than from the single theme or single "figure" of the rose, he arrives not only at an individuation and classification of literary topoi but at a sense of the evolution in a genre of poetry of a topos that sometimes becomes a little plot in miniature, a miniscule allegorical fable with the rose as protagonist. The exceptional development of the stereotype of the rose between the sixteenth and seventeenth centuries is associated with the general phenomenon of Mannerism, from which there also derives a specific and astonishing socioliterary situation: the high consumption and rapid circulation of poety in closed literary circles where an elegant play on the sumptuous variations on a theme takes place.

The process of the transformation of a genre that we have described may justly be called innovative, so that even the transformation may have a regulatory power. The situation is different when a great writer causes a crisis in the constitutive laws of the genre, of its codification. Doubrovsky observes, in speaking of the relation of Racine with the tragic genre, that the great writer does not work in virtue of a law proper to the literary genre that is offered him by literary history; this law, that is, is not accepted by him as a principle of interpretation but as something that in itself has to be interpreted.[27] It becomes part of the general project of the true creator. He becomes for others an incandescent reality: he burns up the past and illuminates the future in flashes, he destroys the norms and allows us to glimpse new ones, if he does not actually institutionalize them in his own work.

For example, within the chivalric genre we can watch two types of action at work: a great writer, Ariosto, who brings the genre to a high level of perfection by transforming it internally, and Cervantes, whose deviations are such as to produce a revolutionary effect. Ariosto's method with regard to the chivalric genre, and in particular to the model offered by Boiardo, is not one of violent break but of shifts in levels; in effect, he reinterprets the law of that literary genre. The first shift is in the factor of construction that links the thematic and formal levels, that is, the key in which the chivalric material is to be read. From the *cantari* (poems) to Boiardo the narration of chivalric events had taken place, in the history of Italian literature, on a lower level than that of an aulic genre like the lyric. The more democratic nature of the chivalric genre, designed for a larger public, was expressed both on the level of the thematic organization (paratactic narrative structure, that is, a linear progression in the narration with subordinate inserts or occurrences) and on the linguistic level, where demotic speech and the presence of regionalisms were the perfect formal correlative of the narrative structure. That is, before Ariosto, the two levels not only were perfectly related in the chivalric genre but seemed to be related *motu proprio* for the very codification of the genre; in fact, Boiardo, who is an authentic, fascinating artist, never transgresses these rules of the game. Ariosto does, and after him there will be no turning back: the rules of the game change with him. Ariosto achieves a coaxial shift in levels—thematic-symbolic, rhythmic, rhetorical, linguistic (the models of Bembo)—by which *Orlando furioso,* without abandoning the chivalric genre, rises in the literary hierarchy to the same nobility as the lyric genre. Ariosto has not broken with the models but has entered into a play of force with them, a "wager" to use Contini's term,[28] to transform the chivalric narrative octave into the lyric without renouncing the narrative character and the secret order beneath the narrative variety, which is revealed gradually in the equilibrium of fantastic additions and ironic subtractions.

For the problem in the literary genre we have been discussing, it happens that in *Orlando furioso,* as so often is the case in masterpieces, characters, themes, and motifs are not new; what is new is the writer's compelling the genre to fulfill its original role as a human emblem.

With Cervantes the offense to the laws of the chivalric genre is so basic and structural that the outcome threatens to destroy the code. Segre observes: "Don Quixote is a kind of gallery of the literary genres of its time; the chivalric romance, although in a parodic key, consisting in part in a resort to the schemes of the picaresque romance; and then the pastoral genre, the adventure novel, the novella, the literary dialogue; and one should not forget love poetry, an element common to both the insertions and adventures of Don Quixote (while only these latter document the popular genre of the *romances*)."[29] Cervantes has deliberately set side by side, without annihilating them, the typical traits of the various genres in a subversive mixture of codes—a death knell for the chivalric genre.

To conclude, whether a great writer guides the imperfect toward perfection, or whether he breaks all the rules of the game, something in the literary system, not only in a genre, will have changed after him. This is the artist's wager with the society of his readers.

## 6. RESTORATIONS AND RECOVERIES

From what has just been said, it may be deduced that, within the transsentential unity of the work, the violations and disruptions of the codification of the genre or of the literary system become the constructive elements of the law of the work. In that case, more disruption equals more artistic information. In a larger context, an analogous phenomenon exists when a group of writers look for more freedom and novelty. These writers turn their backs on the literary system (considered synchronically), and produce, through their violations, a change of relations in the system. That is, they produce something that is from the beginning extremely informative in relation to that macroscopic sign—as Eco would say—which is literature, a sign that communicates the specific character of the sociocultural situation of an era.[30] In this regard, the process that has been noted above in section 2(c) is relevant: that of reinstating a genre after its having been for long at zero point.

We shall take an example from contemporary Italian literature. There are a few writers, in other ways so dissimilar, who in the years 1967–1970 worked on a common and difficult project—Giorgio Manganelli, Alice Ceresa, Sebastiano Vassalli.[31] Their work consisted not only of a negation of the novel genre but, more interestingly, of their attempt to pass beyond the current Italian literary system. Following Vittorini's belief that the nineteenth-century literary experience is a closed circle, these writers went behind Romanticism, that is, they shifted the areas of pertinence: their models are chosen from the orbit of sixteenth- and seventeenth-century Mannerism. This operation is not casual, as we can see from several cultural symptoms; we all know in how many ways the restless seventeenth century is able to speak to us. For example, we may look at linguistic and grammatical theories, or criticism (essays on seventeenth-century artistic phenomena are clearly on the increase), or the semiological field (the rereading, for example, of

Marino and Tesauro), or even at other indices of renewed interest on the thematic-creative level: travel literature in the form of memoirs.

This phenomenon allows us a more general reflection on the dynamics of the literary system: in the literary field as opposed to the field of language, the processes of development do not coincide simply with the diachronic process; there exists in literature *a reversibility of the diachronic*. Baldly put: we cannot speak, except for individual caprice, in the language of the seventeenth century, but we can write in it. Such a recovery also has its law: the reassumption of a literary genre of the past can take place when the opposite phenomenon, that is, its rejection, ceases to be artistically active, productive, or significant in the system. In the Romantic period, a rejection of Mannerism with a Baroque stamp was artistically active; our recovery of Mannerism today is therefore also a negation of that which immediately precedes us in the literary system. It is at least proof of a crisis in the system (though the value of the new experiments would require a separate discourse).

It is significant that when these books first appeared, critics made wide use of the terms "metanovel," "essay novel," and this tells us that there was a more or less conscious tendency to report on these texts as belonging to the area of the codification operating in the system, to assign them to a habitual genre, the novel. But because these texts are not novels, the use of the label "metanovel" redirects the decoding of the addressee, leaving the real operation, that is, the change of the pertinent literary zone, in the shadows. Recovery therefore is not restoration, but renewal of a genre, the result of a program of demystification; literature is an unending concatenation of structures utilized in differing ways.

The choice of the didactic-treatise genre obviously has wide structural implications. Missing is any kind of character (*actant* or simple actor) since the eventual pronoun *we* has the sole function of carrying along the discourse; missing is the temporal category because the argument is in itself atemporal. Lacking characters, action, and time, there is no *récit*, no narrative. The link that binds these texts to the avant-garde is not the deformation of referential reality, but its exclusion; we are in an environmental and historic void, hence the importance of the formal level as the constructive level of the texts. *Nuovo commento* by Giorgio Manganelli is represented as a treatise, an organism commenting on the universe considered as a text, with coequal sounds and linguistic signs—and not as another reality. *La figlia prodiga* by Alice Ceresa is a cold treatise on behavioral logic; the author establishes hypothetical parents and a hypothetical prodigal daughter and examines abstractly the combinatorial game of the possible situations and relations. Echoes of distant literary models may be found in the chapter headings: *Some Stories, Some Characters, Of Prodigality, Where One Meets the Person, On the Dangers of Differentiating Oneself,* etc. *Tempo di massacro* by Sebastiano Vassalli, a book with a Voltairian sneer, is a tract on the theme of destruction as the only form of encounter of the human biped: massacre of one against one, of one against a group, of a people against a people, of poetic guerrilla warfare, and so on. The desacralizing theme of the three books confers a clearly satiric function on the didactic-treatise form. And the counterparts on the level of formal expression are three long scribal ceremonies that have as their base the prefabricated structure of an argument, the Classical *argumentatio* accompanied by the *amplificatio per incrementum,* which is developed through a predominant recourse to parallelism and antithesis. The result is that the syntax, and therefore the style, of the three works is constructed in a coherently binary way; there are two registers of writing, and their interlocking is a constant in the three treatises. The first register presents an isosyntactic structuring of the argumentation with the inventory aspect having the privileged position—a kind of ritualistic syntax, built upon parallelism. Developing inside this large transsentential grid is what Damaso Alonso, speaking of

Mannerist prose, calls an accumulation of nonprogressive syntactic sequences.[32] In Alonso's study, the register of Mannerist
writing is constructed of ramified syntactic sequences, which
are therefore nonprogressive, like the flow of a river that opens
fanlike on the plain instead of running directly toward the river
mouth. The polygenesis of the river image is suggestive for
seventeenth-century prose since even Daniello Bartoli in
*Dell'uomo di lettere* expresses himself with an analogous fantasy:
"Finally, when there is a need for serious talk in order to con-
vince, to rebuke, to condemn an action or a vice or a person, a
style that sings instead of thundering, that instead of tossing
lightning bolts, tosses every which way, like the squirts from a
fountain, sentences that should flow like a stream—every one
can see how far such a style is from achieving its intentions."[33]
There is, we see, a full fidelity in our contemporary examples to
the rules of thematic-formal interaction of seventeeth-century
treatise models; and so we are dealing with a vital recovery.
Notwithstanding this fact, we are not dealing with a simply
mimetic act, because the development of a particular formal
technique is more profound than that. If what Lotman writes is
true, and "every new text rests on elements that are not new;
its newness derives from the form of organization and can be
perceived only comparatively, that is, in confrontation with the
known,"[34] then from that confrontation we notice that there is
no redundancy with respect to seventeenth-century models of
our texts. These new texts, whose artistic quality certainly
needs evaluation (and this would be valid also for other texts
not considered here), are informative from several points of
view: they raise doubts about the contemporary literary system, whose crisis their very existence announces; they bear
witness to the new ideological function of treatise structures
that have been chosen for subtly ironic ends; and on the formal
level, they are polemical alternatives to the ordinary language
of communication that tends to become standardized and prefabricated. This is especially true of Manganelli and Vassalli,

whose lexical, metaphorical, and metonymic exuberance, in the manner of Marino or Rabelais, is played off against their Manneristic syntax. Therefore the linguistic-stylistic level, as a global signifier, constitutes its own meaning (IV.2); it is a large structure symbolic of the message expressed on the thematic level. The message in this case is a rather desacralizing one: it is doubtful whether the world makes any sense, but the writer is the man who spares no effort to overcome obstacles that he knows are insuperable. In saying this, he represents a social conscience.

It should be made clear that we are not dealing here with the epigones of Gadda; the literary operation is very different here, even though these writers would certainly subscribe to Gadda's affirmation: "It may be that the mania for order constrains some to prune the plant of all the capricious branches of liberality and luxury. I, however, declare that I do not belong to any pruning fraternity."[35] An emphatic note may be added to this discourse: the famous literary language, which is traditional, rhetorical, elitist—and as such, contested—can live its most memorable adventure on the plane of literary communication if it is carefully adjusted to demolish the standard of the ordinary communicative canon, if it offers yeast for further disobedience and invention. Zamjatin wrote[36] that scientists have demonstrated that the time has come to stop dividing matter into solids, liquids and gases; there are matter and antimatter. In the same way it makes no sense to speak of artificial and unartificial writers—there are only writers and nonwriters. The activity of the first goes beyond literature; they are never transformed, like Lot's wife, into pillars of salt.

The phenomenon of recovery may come about in a most subtle way inside a genre when, because of particular conditions in the culture, authors jump over a series of links and make use of old models offered by the genre itself. A typical example is the Petrarchism of the seventeenth century that overarches Bembo and, with the possible mediation of French models, attaches itself to a certain Manneristic Petrarchism of the fifteenth century, so that, with an inversion of historical direction, it has been possible to speak of the Baroqueness of fifteenth-century poetry. The analogies between the two groups of texts are thematic, structural, linguistic, and metric.

We have not concerned ourselves in this volume with the problem mentioned in (d) of the scheme of V.2, that is, with the possible formalization based on a homogeneous corpus, for two reasons. The first is that such an operation is still premature, because we still lack that complex of study and textual analysis which leads finally to the process of the "reduction" of the models for a determined corpus. The second is that a similar kind of investigation may be fruitful in a strictly theoretical perspective, but not in the historic-semiological perspective emphasized in this volume.

# Conclusion

The foreword to this work contained a constellation of contradictory or negative definitions of its very object of inquiry—literature; so that the inquiry itself seemed almost impracticable. Perhaps at this point it is possible to emphasize how negation and contradiction result from the fact that literature is in itself a dialectical reality; it lives on conservative forces and on centrifugal thrusts through which the past is destroyed or changes its identity. Nevertheless, a complete diachronic view of literary phenomena reconstitutes a series of connections—beyond any momentary or apparent breaks—of deep or superficial linkings that give a regulating power to the process of transformations; and this allows us to define literature as a dynamic system, a continuity within the discontinuous, a restructuring of that which has undergone dispersal.

We tried then to investigate literature from the perspective of semiotics; every era produces its own type of signedness, which is made manifest in social and literary models. As soon as these models are consumed and reality seems to vanish, new signs become needed to recapture reality, and this allows us to assign an information-value to the dynamic structures of literature. So seen, literature is both the condition and the place of artistic communication between senders and addressees, or public. The messages travel along its paths, in time, slowly or rapidly; some of the messages venture into encounters that undo an entire line of communication; but after great effort a new line will be born. This last fact is the most significant; it requires apprenticeship and dedication on the part of those who would understand it, because the hypersign function of great literary works transforms the grammar of our view of the world.

But the connective tissue of literature is to be found in the minor authors whose texts are coordinated inside the literary genres. These genres are the great institutions that act as mediators between collective consciousness and social structures on the one hand and works of the highest level on the other. In literature nothing is simple, the simple being only our simplification; the study of minor writers yields stimulating results in that their story is the story of literary society and of its rich colloquy that is literature. In considering the relations between works and literary genres we arrived at the notion of code as the canon of interaction between two specific levels, or two spheres—the form of the content and the form of the expression. The hierarchy of codes and their formal strategies are the base of literary language; and we have sustained the right of literary language to claim justly the title of the real alongside ordinary language.

But the history of letters, like that other history, sometimes seems not to know what it is doing. There are the so-called moments of crisis in which there can be glimpsed with singular clarity the connections that link social facts to the life and death of literary institutions. In the course of this work, the contemporary situation has offered us various illuminating examples of this; I note here only the significant change in areas of pertinence, the areas of literary genres and of rhetoric, that is, the fall of both these areas from the upper level of literature, and their extraordinary increment on the level of the mass media and consumer literature. The results have been, on the one hand, romantic stories in the popular magazines, detective stories, historical or other novels scripted for television, stories included in advertising copy, stories in weeklies rigorously codified according to the social class of the addressees—all texts that unquestionably symbolize everything that has disappeared. On the other hand, we have the explosion of rhetorical structures in the messages of special sectors (advertising, politics, sports, etc.). The design of perpetuating certain conventions of the literary system by extending them to areas where a resistance on the part of the addressees does not yet exist, is a countercultural thrust reactionary in nature that has its genesis in extraliterary considerations but that has nonetheless shifted the axis of the literary system. There is always a way, therefore, to demonstrate up to what point literature depends on the nonliterary; it is more difficult to decipher whether what is happening is, finally, a sunset or a dawn.

# Notes

## 1. LITERATURE AND COMMUNICATION

1. Eliot, 1951, p. 15; the essay dates from 1917.

2. Genette, 1966, pp. 165–166. See also Adorno, 1970, p. 445, on the non-necessity of the work before its birth.

3. Kristeva, 1970, pp. 139–146.

4. Corti, 1968, regarding the second edition of *Arcadia* by Jacobo Sannazaro.

5. Borges, 1960, p. 148; English translation, p. 108. Borges refers to—but does not quote directly—Eliot in his footnote 2: "See T.S. Eliot, *Points of View* (1941), pp. 25–26."

6. Avalle, 1975.

7. Gadda, 1974, p. 259.

8. The relations established by Escarpit, 1968, pp. 29–40, are somewhat superficial. For a history of the structuralist concepts of literature, but in its linguistic aspects only, see Ihwe, 1973, pp. 31–44.

9. Wienold, 1972.

10. Gadda, 1974, p. 229.

11. The process is masterfully illustrated by Mukařovský, 1966.

12. In *Littérature et Société*, 1967, p. 54. Hobsbawm, 1974, p. 13, emphasizes that "for the greater part of history we are facing societies and communities for whom the past is essentially the model for the present"; so that innovation, maturing within the interstices of the conscious system, is accepted peacefully.

13. Schücking, 1923, p. 12; English translation, p. 3.

14. Some interesting statistics with percentages are treated by Escarpit, in *Littérature et Société*, 1967, p. 152.

15. See P. Orecchioni, "Pour une histoire sociologique de la littérature," in *Le Littéraire et le social*, 1970, pp. 43–53.

16. A good perspective is offered here by C. Cases, "La critica sociologica," in *I metodi attuali*, 1970, pp. 23–40, and Golino, 1973; 1974.

17. Corsini, 1974, p. 17.

18. Van Dijk, 1972, pp. 182–184; 339–340.

19. The theory of "social groups" was already approached by Schücking, 1923.

20. Goldmann, 1964. In addition, the important essay "Le structuralisme génétique en sociologie de la littérature," in *Littérature et Société*, 1967, pp. 195–222.

21. In *Littérature et Société*, 1967, pp. 47–71.

22. Gallas, 1971, pp. 103–116. Useful insights are in F. Camon, *Letterature e classi subalterne*, Padua, Marsilio, 1974.

23. Jauss, 1967, pp. 26–28. Duchet, 1971, pp. 5–14.

24. Zambardi, 1973, p. 12.

25. Rossi-Landi, 1972, p. 107.

26. "Pour une critique littéraire sociologique," in *Le littéraire et le social*, 1970, pp. 55–75.

27. H. Zalamansky, "L'étude des contenus, étage fondamentale de la sociologie de la littérature contemporaine," in *Le littéraire et le social*, 1970, pp. 119–128; M.C. Albrecht, "Does Literature Reflect Common Values," in *American Sociological Review*, XXI, 1956, pp. 722–729.

28. Zambardi, 1973, p. 75.

29. Escarpit, in *Littérature et Société*, 1967, pp. 22–23: ". . . personally I associated myself with the sociology of literature to rid myself of the notions about the work and its creator that have blocked literary thought for too long. That is why I have replaced, in my terminology, the notion of the work with the notion of the *literary fact*. The literary fact is the exchange, the communication, the movement of the author to the public." See also Silbermann, in the same text, p. 42.

30. In this perspective, various threads of Marxist and dialectical criticism are present, for which see Gallas, 1971; Cases, "La critica sociologica," in *I metodi attuali*, 1970; Jameson, 1971; for a more recent bibliography, see the issue of the review, *Problemi*, edited by G. Petronio. The ideological-political attitude in critical theory associated with historical materialism is all-pervasive in treating all of western art as bourgeois (as in Luperini, 1971) and opposing to it the "boundless revolutionary subject" (Luperini, 1971, pp. 90–91). This approach is so general that it is hardly productive for specific inquires into literary processes. In the Italian context, a place apart must be made for the studies of Italian literature based on a profundly different and insightful ideological approach by Sebastiano Timpanaro and Franco Fortini.

31. Mukařovský, 1966, p. 146.

32. J. Lotman, "Il problema del segno e del sistema segnico nella tipologia della cultura russa prima del XX secolo," in *Ricerche*

*semiotiche*, 1973, pp. 40–63. D.S. Lichačëv, "Le proprietà dinamiche dell'ambiente nelle opere letterarie (Per una impostazione del problema)," ibid., pp. 26-39.

33. Auerbach, 1946, p. 77.

34. The work edited in *Bibliotheca Maxima Patrum*, vol. XXV, Lyons, 1677, has been the object of recent study, in relation to medieval philosophy, by Carla Casagrande, *La teoria della predicazione domenicana di Umberto da Romans. Sociologia e valori* (still unpublished thesis directed by the medievalist Franco Alessio at the University of Pavia, 1975).

35. Casagrande, thesis, 1975, p. 225.

36. Fabbri, 1973, pp. 57–109; Eco, 1976, pp. 289–297.

37. Gombrich, "Psychoanalysis and the History of Art," in 1963, pp. 30–44, especially p. 35.

## II. SENDER AND ADDRESSEE
### IIa. The Sender

1. Lotman, 1970, p. 15.

2. "Le temps retrouvé," in Proust, 1954, p. 696.

3. Terminology taken from Chatman, 1974, p. 3.

4. Blanchot, 1955, p. 12.

5. E. Vittorini, *Le opere narrative*, edited by M. Corti, Milan, Mondadori, 1974, pp. xii–xiii and passim.

6. I wish to thank General Piero Ghiacci ("Pierre" of *Partigiano Johnny*) for having allowed me to consult the personal dossier of partisan Fenoglio in the Ministry of Defense. It will be reproduced in the Einaudi edition of the published and unpublished *Opere* where *l'Ur Partigiano Johnny* will appear.

7. Gadda, 1974, pp. 37; 72.

8. Mounin, 1969, p. 279.

9. Foucault, 1971, pp. 10–20.

10. Chatman, 1974, p. 3.

11. Todorov, 1971, p. 40; also in the chapter, "Le récit comme procès d'énonciation." Kristeva, 1970, on the double status of the *destinateur*, pp. 98–104.

12. Foucault, 1971, p. 20.

13. Starobinski, 1970, pp. 257–341.

14. Gramigna, 1975, p. 125. In polemic with the analogy and homology of dream and work cf. Gombrich, 1963, pp. 30–44; and p. 43: "The point is that he [the artist] has found himself in a situation in which his private conflicts acquired artistic relevance. Without the

social factors, what we may term the attitudes of the audience, the style or the trend, the private needs could not be transmuted into art. In this transmutation the private meaning is all but swallowed up."

15. Jakobson, 1973, in the chapter, "Structures linguistiques sub-liminales en poésie," pp. 280–292. See also Dragonetti, 1969.

16. See the incisive studies of Agosti, 1972; F. Orlando, *Lettura freudiana della Phedre*, Turin, Einaudi, 1971. In addition, cf. Orlando, 1973, about whom see the reflections of E. Benevelli, "Su letteratura, psicanalisi e marxismo," in *Strumenti critici*, 27, 1975, pp. 241–252; Barberi Squarotti, "Stile impulso biologico inconscio," in Barberi Squarotti, 1972, pp. 67–92. A place apart is occupied in the Italian context by the group of the review, *Il piccolo Hans* (C. Calligaris, S. Finzi, Virginia Finzi Ghisi, E. Krumm), whose work is in the Lacan and ideological area. The extensive French bibliography is well known. For the Italian, cf. M. David, "La critica psicanalitica," in *I metodi attuali*, 1970, pp. 115–123. Also see David's entry, "Psicanalisi e letterature," in *Dizionario critico della letteratura italiana*, Turin, UTET, 1974, where reference is made to the numerous works of David himself.

17. G. Leopardi, *Entro dipinta gabbia. Tutti gli scritti inediti, rari e editi 1809–1810*, edited by M. Corti, Milan, Bompiani, 1972.

18. Lacan, 1972, p. 37.

19. Leopardi, *Entro dipinta gabbia*, pp. 405–406.

20. Jakobson, 1963, pp. 220–223.

21. *Delle Opere del P. Daniello Bartoli, Le Morali*, Rome, Stamperia del Varese, MDCLXXXIV, pp. 224–225.

22. Zanzotto, 1973 (the pages are unnumbered).

23. Eliot, 1951[3], p. 30; the essay dates from 1923.

24. See N. Jitrik, "Structure et signification de *Fictions* de J.L. Borges," in *Linguistique et littérature*, Colloque de Cluny, *La Nouvelle Critique*, Numéro spécial, 1968, pp. 107–114, especially p. 113: "In *Fictions* he has chosen an alternative, while protesting against the fact of having to lay aside all the other alternatives and seeing himself obliged to recount that one. Macheray ('Pour une théorie de la prod-uction littéraire') understands this drama of Borges: 'How to write the simplest story, when it implies the possibility of infinite variations, where the chosen form will always *lack* the other forms that could have been there?'"

25. Ihwe, 1970; 1973, pp. 42–43. Van Dijk, 1972, pp. 170, 228–308.

26. For the grammar of poetic competence, see the comment on Bierwisch in IIIb.4.

27. In *Le littéraire et le social*, 1970, p. 30.

28. Greimas, 1966.

29. Chatman, 1974, p. 3.

**IIb. The Addressee**

1. Ch. J. Rychner, *La chanson de geste. Essai sur l'art épique des jongleurs*, Geneva, 1955. Zumthor, 1972, pp. 37-42, where a certain parallel between medieval oral diffusion and today's mass media may be noted.

2. Segre, 1974, pp. 6–7.

3. In *Poétique*, 14, 1973, pp. 178–196.

4. Zumthor, 1972, pp. 31–36.

5. Auerbach, 1958, pp. 225–238.

6. G. Vasari, *Le Vite de più eccellenti pittori scultori e architettori*, in the editions of 1550 and 1568, text edited by Rosanna Bettarini. Variorum commentary edited by Paola Barocchi, vol. III, Florence, Sansoni, 1971, p. 5.

7. Kris, 1952, pp. 13–84. Gombrich, 1963, pp. 35–36.

8. Foucault, "Che cos'è un autore?" in Foucault, 1971, pp. 3, 6.

9. Blanchot, 1955, p. 256.

10. Mukařovský, 1966, p. 187. Chatman, 1974, p. 28.

11. Sartre, 1947–1949, pp. 130–133 in *Situations II*.

12. Blanchot, 1955, p. 271: every reading is spoken of as a "unique reading, that each time is the first and only"; on the reader-text struggle see also pp. 263–278.

13. Gramigna, 1975, above all, the first twenty pages.

14. Auerbach, 1946, pp. 115-117, 160-168, 497; Lichačëv, in *Ricerche semiotiche*, 1973, pp. 26–39; Zumthor, 1972, p. 31.

15. On the distinction between the lay and clerical public and on the groups of addressees for certain literary genres rather than others, see Delbouille, 1970; Auerbach, 1958, pp. 224–225.

16. See G. Mury, "Sociologie du public littéraire: le concept de personnalité de base et la convergence des procédures de recherche," in *Le littéraire et le social*, 1970, pp. 205–220.

17. Escarpit and Robine, 1963; Wienold, 1972, p. 175.

18. Escarpit, in *Le littéraire et le social*, 1970, p. 25.

19. Zumthor, 1972, p. 20.

20. Until now there have been very few careful studies on the role of social, professional, and economic differences in regard to the reading of literature that would correspond to what is being done in sociolinguistics in regard to language; see, for example, W. Labov,

"The Reflection of Social Process in Linguistic Structures," in *Readings in the Sociology of Language*, Mouton, The Hague, 1968. On the advanced level of sociolinguistic research and its influence on the literary field, see no. 11, 1968, of the review *Langages:* "Sociolinguistique," edited by J. Sumpf. In addition, a social history of literature on the diachronic level must take into account the physical means of transmission and transform itself at some point into a social history of writing, with the contribution of special disciplines. No history of literature has as yet taken account of the means of transmission of texts, nor offered statistics, where possible, of the diffusion of works, as if the life of a work were not strongly conditioned by such extraliterary factors. One thinks of the kind of circulation of manuscripts in medieval culture over vast geographic space but in a single social stratum or else of the passing of the same manuscript through many hands and collections with the layers of notes and comments, a phenomenon of great importance in literary history that may be associated with practical and economic reasons. The invention of printing has unusual consequences in the text-addressee relation and provokes particularly noteworthy events through the centuries. For example, Stendhal, that attentive observer of literary consumption, notes (1956, pp. 700–714, article of 1832) that the success of a book depends in part on its format: "But to obtain this mark of success it is indispensable that the book be printed in octavo format," so that if by chance it is in duodecimo it is understood by the public to be a novel for *femmes de chambre*. What connotes a book today is, in part, its cover. Pertinent observations in Lefebvre, 1966, pp. 46–47; Escarpit, 1968, pp. 17–21, 61–71; Corsini, 1974, passim.

21. Jauss, 1967, chaps. VI–XII on the phenomenon of reception; Weinrich, 1967.

22. Riffaterre, 1972, p. 15.

23. Wienold, 1972, chap. III.

24. Genette, 1966, pp. 158–159.

25. Starobinski, 1965, pp. xix–xx.

26. 1970, p. 10.

27. 1969; and, in addition, in the article "La Productivité dite texte," in *Communications*, 11, 1968, pp. 59–83.

28. 1970, pp. 33–39.

29. 1967, p. 49; the article dates from 1921.

30. 1966, pp. 51–54.

31. Sartre, 1947–1949, p. 118 in *Situations II*.

32. Valéry, I, 1442.

33. R. Estival, "Création, consommation et production intellectuelles," in *Le littéraire et le social*, 1970, pp. 165–205, on p. 169.

34. Auerbach, 1946, pp. 230–231, 272–273, 324–325.

35. Stendhal, 1952, pp. 700–703, 713.

## III.   THE LINGUISTIC SPACE
### IIIa.  Language and Literary Language

1. For the concept of supersign-function see Eco, 1976, pp. 261–273, especially p. 271.

2. Van Dijk, 1972, p. 200. See also Ihwe, 1973, pp. 37–50. On the noncoextensiveness of poetic function in the language and in poetic language see IIIb.3.

3. Barthes, 1966, the entire discussion on pp. 56–63. On *poétique* as *science du discours* see Todorov, 1967, p. 8.

4. Granger, 1968, pp. 191–192.

5. Van Dijk, 1972, p. 199.

6. *Rimario* was published in A. Porta, *Week-end*, with a foreword by M. Corti, Rome, Cooperativa degli scrittori, 1974; A. Zanzotto, "Rime per l'io fantasma," *Corriere della Sera*, 10 August 1975.

7. S. Debenedetti, "Le canzoni di Stefano Protonatoro: P. I. La canzone siciliana," in *Studi Romanzi*, XXII, 1932, pp. 5–68, on p. 36.

8. *I linguaggi settoriali*, 1973; *Italiano d'oggi*, 1974.

9. Riffaterre, 1960.

10. Blanchot, 1955, p. 37.

11. Lefebvre, 1966, p. 371. See also Rossi-Landi, 1972, pp. 201–204.

12. J. Onimus, "Ruptures et interférences dans le langage poétique," in *Degrés*, 2, 1973, pp. e1–e9, alludes perhaps to something analogous when he writes: "We know how poetic writing liberated itself from the *carcan* of rules to get closer to oral, emotional language, which is undoubtedly its original language."

13. M. Wandruszka, "La lingua quale polisistema socioculturale," in *Italiano d'oggi*, 1974, pp. 3–17.

14. Auerbach, 1946, p. 127.

15. Barthes, 1953, p. 34. On the stylistic theories of Barthes see Barberi Squarotti, 1972, pp. 21–22.

16. Wandruszka, in *Italiano d'oggi*, 1974, p. 12.

17. Eco, 1976, pp. 276–289. For a history and bibliography of rhetoric see Fischer, 1973, pp. 134–156. In addition, see U. Florescu, *La retorica nel suo sviluppo storico*, Bologna, il Mulino, 1971 (the work in the original Rumanian dates from 1960); G. Preti, *Retorica e logica: le*

*due culture*, Turin, Einaudi, 1968; R. Barilli, *Poetica e retorica*, Milan, Mursia, 1968; C. Vasoli, "La 'nouvelle rhétorique' di Perelman," in *Attualità della retorica*, 1975, pp. 13–36; R. Barilli, "Retorica e narrativa," in *Attualità della retorica*, 1975, pp. 37–54; R. Baehr, "Retorica rediviva?" in *Attualità della retorica*, 1975, pp. 89–100. Cf. also Jacques Dubois, F. Edeline, J.M. Klinkenberg, P. Minguet, F. Pire, H. Trinon, *Rhétorique générale*, Paris, Larousse, 1970.

18. Garavelli Mortara, 1974, p. 33.

19. *Languaggi settoriali*, 1974, and especially the essay by Eco on the language of politicians. For the increase in the conative function see M. Corti, "Per una nuova prospettiva nello studio del linguaggio pubblicitario," in *Italiano d'oggi*, 1974, pp. 57–58.

20. R. Barthes, "L'analyse rhétorique," in *Littérature et Société*, 1967, pp. 30–45.

21. Cohen, 1966, p. 46.

22. Genette, 1969, pp. 138–139.

23. Van Dijk, 1973, p. 249.

24. In *Mathematik und Dichtung*, 1965, pp. 275–293; the citation is on p. 279.

25. Corti, 1968.

26. Corti, 1956, pp. xli–xlix.

27. Gadda, 1958, p. 78.

28. From a forthcoming publication by Silvia Isella.

29. See Introduction by D. Isella to C. Porta, *Poesie*, Milan, Mondadori, 1975.

30. Milan, Mondadori, 1975.

31. Auerbach, 1946, p. 180.

32. Petrocchi, 1969, pp. 244–245.

33. Mandelstam, 1967, p. 137.

34. Guglielmi, 1974: on *antiletteratura*, pp. 16–21; the citation is on p. 16. See also Guglielmi, 1967: the chapter "Idea e ideologia della letteratura moderna."

35. M. Corti, "La lingua e gli scrittori, oggi," In Corti, 1969, pp. 93–108 (the article dates from 1965).

### IIIb.  The Distinctiveness of Poetic Language

1. Cohen, 1966, pp. 9–11.

2. Zamjatin, 1970, pp. 67–68.

3. Terracini, 1966, pp. 209–249. On the problem of the prose-poetry relation see Avalle, 1974, pp. 12–23. Van Dijk, 1972, pp. 281–283.

4. Lotman, 1970, pp. 120–131.

5. Mandelstam, 1967, p. 148 (the essay dates from the Thirties).

6. Freudian psychoanalytical criticism would substitute, for the psychic process of the Indian theorists, memory traces linked to the psychic activity of recollection.

7. Valéry, I, p. 1338.

8. In Jakobson, 1973, p. 133. See also Proust, 1954, pp. 718–719.

9. Char, 1957, p. 199.

10. Agosti, 1972, p. 43.

11. Coseriu, 1962; but see especially Van Dijk, 1972, and the references given in IIIa.1.

12. See Genette, 1969, pp. 151–152, when in reference to *Le poème du haschisch*, part IV, he observes the planetary distance of this conception from the "poetry of grammar" of Jakobson.

13. Lotman, 1970, p. 114.

14. A text may actually have a figure as its generative structure, and even a prosaic text (Todorov, 1971, p. 35).

15. Mallarmé, 1945, p. 366.

16. Mandelstam, 1967, p. 44; the article dates from 1921.

17. Benn, 1959, 4, p. 1070.

18. Luzi, 1974, p. 37.

19. Mandelstam, 1967, p. 43.

20. J.M. Klinkenberg, "Vers un modèle théorique du langage poétique," in *Degrés*, 1, 1973, dd–12.

21. Again, the expression is from Char, 1957, p. 204.

22. Agosti, 1972, p. 52.

23. Pagnini, 1974, pp. 13–14.

24. Agosti, 1972, pp. 11–43.

25. Serpieri, 1973, p. 41.

26. J. Starobinski in Introduction to R. Char, *Ritorno sopramonte e altra poesia*, Milan, Mondadori, 1974, pp. 9–26; the citation is on pp. 9–10.

27. Jakobson, 1963, p. 220. Originally in English in "Linguistics and Poetics," in *Style and Language*, ed. Thomas A. Sebeok, New York, 1960, p. 358.

28. Todorov, 1971a, pp. 275–286.

29. F. Sabatini, "Il messaggio pubblicitario da slogan a prosa-poesia," in *Il Ponte*, 24, 1968, pp. 3–19.

30. Levin, 1962, p. 41.

31. Mandelstam, 1967, p. 135.

32. Eco, 1976, pp. 261–276, in 3.7.6: "Aesthetic idiolect."

33. Brioschi, 1974, pp. 413–414.

34. Risset, 1972, p. 165.

35. Blanchot, 1965, p. 169.
36. Eco, 1976, p. 261.
36a. Eco, 1975, p. 339.
37. Bierwisch, 1969, pp. 49–65.
38. Zumthor, 1972a, p. 322.
39. Zumthor, 1975, p. 28.
40. Risset, 1972, p. 222.
41. Poe, 1945, p. 550; Benn, 1959, 4, p. 1070.
42. Valéry, 1957, I, p. 1467.
43. Contini, 1970, p. 5: the essay dates from 1942 (but was written in 1941).
43a. Poe, 1945, p. 551.
44. Contini, 1970, pp. 5–31, 42–52, 169–192.
45. Char, 1957, p. 203.
46. Contini, 1970, p. 7.
47. Contini, 1970, pp. 51–52.
48. Mandelstam, 1967, p. 148, in "Discorso su Dante."

## IV.  HYPERSIGN

1. T. Mann, *Adel des Geistes: Sechzehn Versuche zum Problem der Humanität,* Stockholm, 1945; later edition, Berlin and Weimar, 1965, pp. 424–425. See Corti, 1968, p. 141.
2. From an interview with G.G. Márquez in *L'Espresso,* 28, 13 July 1975.
3. Poe, 1945, pp. 549–565 (article dates from 1846).
4. Corti, 1968, pp. 141–167.
5. Benn, 1959, 4, p. 1071.
6. Van Dijk, 1972, pp. 184–188, 273–305.
7. Pagnini, 1974, pp. 41–42. For a thorough study of levels see Pagnini, 1967; Tavani, 1972, especially pp. 22–45.
8. Corti, 1973a, pp. 157–183.
9. From current research on Gadda's manuscripts in the "Manuscript Collection of Contemporary Authors" of the Institute of History of the Italian Language at the University of Pavia.
10. Segre, 1974, pp. 97–99.
11. Agosti, 1972, especially pp. 49–52; Tavani, 1972; Beccaria, 1975.
12. Beccaria, 1975, chapter III on Dante's rhythmemes.
13. Rightly, Beccaria does not accept determinism in the relation between sound and image, as does Fónagy ("Communication in Poetry," in *Word,* XVII, 1961, pp. 194–218), but adds: "The phoneme /i/, which the subject judges as brighter that /u/, may very well be applied by a poet (for example, Baudelaire) to suggest the night ('L' irrésistible nuit établit son empire'); /i/ is in itself unmotivated.

Poetic language confers upon it what it lacks in the *langue,* in Saussure's sense, that is to say, motivation" (1975, p. 75).

14. Agosti, 1972, pp. 15–43, is rich in examples.

15. In *Ricerche semiotiche,* 1973, p. 318.

16. Gadda, 1958, p. 12.

17. Gombrich, 1963, pp. 43–44. The poetic quotation is from Wordsworth's *The Prelude,* 1. I, vv. 341–344.

18. See Brooks, 1947, in the article, "The Heresy of Paraphrase," pp. 176–196. See also IIIb.4.

19. Van Dijk, 1972, about which see V.2; Segre, 1974, pp. 19–20.

20. C.E. Gadda, *La cognizione del dolore,* Turin, Einaudi, 1970, p. 32.

21. In the essay "Belle lettere e contributi delle techniche" (Gadda, 1958, pp. 77–91) the writer uses some typical expressions to indicate the nature of such a program: "The disintegration and the successive and new integration of the raw material must be motivated" (p. 89), "the task of disintergrating and reconstructing the expression" (p. 90), etc.; and for the similarity with the mason: "Let us say that he can grind down the brick offered to him and then reform and reshape it as a brick in his own way, and then proceed to the making of 'his wall,' that is, 'his work'" (p. 88). On the ways of artistic construction see Geninasca, 1972.

22. Eliot, 1964, p. 153.

23. Lotman, 1970, p. 86.

24. Beccaria, 1975, p. 25.

25. D.S. Lichačëv, "Le proprietà dinamiche dell'ambiente nelle opere letterarie," in *Ricerche semiotiche,* pp. 26–39.

26. The most recent and precise analysis of the concepts of plot, *fabula,* and model is to be found in Segre, 1974, pp. 3–72; the notion of "discourse" here seems to include both that of the whole text—completed and legible—and of the formal aspects of that same text. In our treatment of form of the content and form of expression the reference is not to the glossematic approach to literary texts of Trabant, 1970, but rather to the differentiation, in cultural contexts, used by Umberto Eco, 1971.

27. Chatman, 1974, p. 1.

28. "Les relations de temps dans le verbe français," in Benveniste, 1966, pp. 238–245. His observations on the correspondence between literary genres and the use of certain tenses is important.

28a. G. Flaubert, *Correspondances,* II, Paris, Conard, 1926, p. 451: "Les chefs-d'oeuvre sont bêtes; ils ont la mine tranquille comme les productions mêmes de la nature, comme les grands animaux et les montagnes."

29. In *Trattati,* I, 1970, p. 561.

30. Eco, 1962, p. 41.

31. Eco, 1976, p. 271.

32. In *Strumenti critici,* 26, 1975, pp. 80–112. We can now add Ser-pieri, 1975, pp. 13–16.

33. Corti, 1975, pp. 182–197.

34. An excellent example in Avalle, *"Gli orecchini* di Montale" (1965), now in Avalle, 1970, pp. 1–90.

35. Benn, 1959, 4, pp. 1116–1146.

36. See the study of *Soledades* by A. Machado in Segre, 1969, pp. 95–134.

## V. LITERARY GENRES AND CODIFICATION

1. See L. Salviati, *Della poetica lezion prima,* in *Trattati,* II, 1970, p. 592, with reference to Aristotle, *Topica,* VI, 3.

2. Krauss, 1968, pp. 5–44; Jauss, 1970; Hempfer, 1973.

3. Genette, 1966, p. 164; Todorov, 1971, p. 225; Van Dijk, 1972, p. 171 and passim; Hempfer, 1973, p. 62.

4. In *Trattati,* I, II, 1970; III, 1972; IV, 1974.

5. Genot, 1970, p. 14.

6. A detailed study in Hempfer, 1973; for the evolutionary theory, pp. 58–59.

7. Krauss, 1968, p. 6, recounts a curious remark by Ortega y Gas-set in polemic with Croce: "Every poetic work belongs to a genre just as every animal belongs to a species."

8. Lotman, 1970, p. 71.

9. E. Koehler, "Les possiblités de l'interpretation sociologique il-lustrées par l'analyse de textes littéraires français de différentes époques," in *Littérature et Société,* 1967, pp. 49–63, on p. 52.

10. Corti, 1959, on pp. 73–81.

11. Ch. Aubrun, in *Littérature et Société,* 1967, pp. 137–150; Escar-pit, ibid., pp. 146–147. Kristeva, 1970, is concerned with the *processus de mutation* (p. 17), taking from Lukács the concept of the rapid change in the novel genre.

12. Jauss, 1967; Mury in *Le littéraire et le social,* 1970, p. 215; Stem-pel, 1971; Zumthor, 1972, pp. 157–184; Hempfer, 1973, pp. 84–91. This double problem seems to me more productive for cultural history than the opposite approach of Todorov, 1971, p. 255: "Or else we describe the genres 'just as they have existed,' or, more exactly, just as the critical tradition (metaliterary) has consecrated them: the ode or the elegy 'exist' because these designations are found in the critical discourse of a certain era. But then we renounce all hope of construct-

ing a system of genres. Or we start from the fundamental properties of the literary fact and declare that their different combinations produce the genres. In that case we must adhere to a deceiving generality and content ourselves, for example, with the division into lyric, epic, and dramatic; then we find it impossible to explain the absence of a genre that would have the rhythmic structure of the elegy joined to a happy theme. Now the aim of a theory of genres is to explain the system of *existing* genres: why these and not others? The distance between the theory and the description remains irreducible." My answer to Todorov emerges from this chapter; here I would note only the absence in Todorov of a consideration of the sociocultural context of genres as modes of literary communication.

13. *La Poetica*, II, in *Trattati*, I, 1970, p. 44.

14. A concept already in Eco, 1971. In other circles this restriction does not exist; see L. Prieto, *Messages et signaux*, Presses Universitaires de France, 1966.

15. "Poétique," in *Qu'est-ce-que le structuralisme?* 1968, p. 157.

16. I do not use here the notion of program in the sense noted by Hempfer, 1973, pp. 109–110 ("*Gattungen*" as "*Programme*"), which is that of the theory of information.

17. A. Porta, "Una letteratura fuori parcheggio," in *Il Giorno*, 3 September 1975.

18. Corti, 1968, pp. 141–167; Corti, 1972, pp. 11–18.

19. Lausberg, 1949, sections 230, 422, 423–25.

20. See Corti, 1974, for North Italian examples, where the thematic variations of the *nenciale* tradition are nonetheless minimal, in a strict sense; peripherally, there exist texts like the "*canzone*" edited by Patetta, and in reality consisting of four octaves.

21. D. De Robertis' remarks about the ballad he edited are interesting from the point of view of metrics in "Un nuovo 'Ritmo nenciale' in un manoscritto fiorentino della prima età di Lorenzo," in *Studi di filogia italiana*, XXI, 1963, pp. 201–215, on p. 204; "A text apparently less beholden to the form and motif that will make the *Nencia* famous, even though the strophe of hendecasyllables [AA] BCBCCA repeats the movement for quite a way in this regard."

22. See for rustic topoi A. Di Benedetto, "Due note sulla 'Nencia da Barberino,'" in *Atti del Convegno sul tema: La poesia rusticana nel Rinascimento*," Rome, Accademia Nazionale dei Lincei, 1969, pp. 29–41, and the earlier bibliography therein.

23. "Due altri testi della tradizione nenciale," in *Studi di filologia italiana*, XXV, 1967, pp. 109–153.

24. Mukařovský, 1966, p. 33.

25. Risset, 1972, pp. 13–28.

26. Pozzi, 1974.

27. Doubrovsky, 1967, p. 42; English translation, p. 97.

28. Contini, 1974, pp. 231–241 (the essay dates from 1937).

29. Segre, 1974, p. 192.

30. Eco, 1971.

31. Alice Ceresa, *La figlia prodiga*, Turin, Einaudi, 1967; Giorgio Manganelli, *Nuovo commento*, Turin, Einaudi, 1970; Sebastiano Vassalli, *Tempo di massacro*, Turin, Einaudi, 1970. For a broader treatment of this corpus with regard to the rescue of a genre, see Corti, 1973, pp. 93–105.

32. *"Sintagmas no progresivos y pluralidades: Tres calillas en la prosa castellana,"* in *Seis escalas en la expresión literaria española*, Madrid, Gredos, 1951, pp. 23–42.

33. D. Bartoli, *Dell'uomo di lettere*, Rome, MDCXLV[1], in the chapter entitled "Stile fiorito, e troppo ingegnoso."

34. Lotman, 1970.

35. Gadda, 1958, p. 99.

36. Zamjatin, 1970, p. 107. Zamjatin gave the lectures in 1920 in the House of Arts in Petrograd (Leningrad).

# General Bibliography

Not all the works cited in the course of this volume are included in this bibliography, but only those used most frequently or of particular pertinence for this study; for the rest, see the notes. Articles contained in anthologies or works or in collections of various authors are cited in the course of this work with reference to title, date, and page of the collection; in the case of more ample or special use, the specific title of the article is given in the bibliography or the notes. Russian and Czech texts used in translation are cited with the date of the original and the pagination of the Italian translation used. Page references to works in other languages refer to the pagination of the original language edition, unless the original pagination has been supplanted or supplemented by the pagination of the English translation—with clear indications of that in the footnotes, and reference to the English translation in this bibliography. For Valéry, who is cited often, the references have been simplified by citing in Roman numerals the volume of the *Oeuvres* and the page number; Proust is listed with the date and pages of the Gallimard edition. In the case of both Proust and Valéry the edition dates are in parentheses.

ANTHOLOGIES, COLLECTIONS

1965 *Théorie de la littérature*, Paris, Editions du Seuil.

1965 *Mathematik und Dichtung*, Munich, Kreuzer H. u. Gunzenhaüser R. (quoted from the 1969 edition).

1967 *Littérature et Société* ("Colloque organisé conjointement par l'Institut de Sociologie de l'Université Libre de Bruxelles et l'Ecole Pratique des Hautes Etudes de Paris"), Brussels, Editions de l'Institut de Sociologie de l'Université Libre de Bruxelles.

1968 *Qu'est-ce-que le structuralisme?*, Paris, Editions du Seuil.

1970 *I metodi attuali della critica in Italia*, Turin, Edizioni ERI.

1970 *La critica forma caratteristica della civiltà moderna* ("Quaderni di San Girogio," 33), Florence, Sansoni.

1970 *Le littéraire et le social*, Paris, Flammarion.

1973 *Ricerche Semiotiche* ("Nuove tendenze delle scienze umane nell'URSS," edited by J.M. Lotman and B.A. Uspenskij), Turin, Einaudi.

1973 *I linguaggi settoriali*, Milan, Bompiani.

1974 *Italiano d'oggi: Lingua non letteraria e lingue speciali*, Trieste, Lint.

1970–1974 *Trattati di poetica e retorica del '500*, 4 vols., Bari, Laterza (cited as *Trattati*, followed by the number of the volume).

1975 *Attualità della retorica* ("Atti del I Convegno italo-tedesco, Bressanone, 1973"), Padua, Liviana Editrice.


ADORNO, THEODOR W.

1970 *Ästhetische Theorie*, Frankfurt a. M., Suhrkamp (Ital. tr., *Teoria estetica*, Turin, Einaudi, 1975).

AGOSTI, S.

1972 *Il testo poetico: Teoria e pratica d'analisi*, Milan, Rizzoli.

AUERBACH, ERICH

1946 *Mimesis: Dargestellte Wirklichkeit in der Abendländischen Literatur*, Bern, Francke (Eng. tr., *Mimesis: The Representation of Reality in Western Literature*, Garden City, Doubleday, 1957).

1958 *Literatursprache und Publikum in der lateinischen Spätantike und im Mittelalter*, Bern, Francke.

AVALLE, D'ARCO SILVIO

1970 *Tre saggi su Montale*, Turin, Einaudi.

1974 *La poesia nell'attuale universo semiologico*, Turin, Giappichelli.

1975 *Modelli semiologici nella "Commedia" di Dante*, Milan, Bompiani.


BARBERI SQUAROTTI, G.

1972 *Il codice di Babele*, Milan, Rizzoli.

BARTHES, ROLAND

1953 *Le degré zéro de l'écriture*, Paris, Editions du Seuil (Eng. tr., *Writing Degree Zero*, New York, Hill & Wang, 1968).

1966 *Critique et Vérité*, Paris, Editions du Seuil.

1970 *S/Z*, Paris, Editions du Seuil (Eng. tr., *S/Z*, New York, Hill & Wang, 1974).

1973 *Le plaisir du texte*, Paris, Editions du Seuil (Eng. tr., *The Pleasure of the Text*, New York, Hill & Wang, 1975).

BECCARIA, G. L.

1975 *L'autonomia del significante*, Turin, Einaudi.

BENN, GOTTFRIED

1959 *Gesammelte Werke*, 8 vols.: vol. 3, *Essays und Aufsätze*; vol. 4, *Reden und Vorträge*, Wiesbaden, Limes.

BENVENISTE, EMILE
1966 *Problèmes de linguistique générale*, Paris, Gallimard.
BIERWISCH, MANFRED
1965 "Poetik und Linguistik," in *Mathematik und Dichtung* (quoted from the 1969 edition, pp. 49–65).
BLANCHOT, MAURICE
1955 L'espace littéraire, Paris, Gallimard.
BORGES, JORGE LUIS
1960 *Otras inquisiciones*, Buenos Aires, Emecé (Eng. tr., *Other Inquisitions*, Austin, University of Texas Press, 1964).
BRIOSCHI, FRANCESCO
1974 "Il lettore e il testo poetico," in *Comunità*, 173, pp. 365–417.
BROOKS, CLEANTH
1947 *The Well Wrought Urn: Studies in the Structure of Poetry*, New York, Harcourt, Brace and World.

CHAR, RENÉ
1957 *Partage formel* (1942), in *Poèmes et Proses*, Paris, Gallimard.
CHATMAN, SEYMOUR
1974 "La struttura della comunicasione letteraria," in *Strumenti critici*, 23, pp. 1–40 (essay translated from the English of a volume-in-progress, *Story and Discourse*, to be published by Cornell University Press).
COHEN, JEAN
1966 *Structure du langage poétique*, Paris, Flammarion.
CONTINI, GIANFRANCO
1970 *Varianti e altra linguistica: Una raccolta di saggi (1938–1968)*, Turin, Einaudi.
1972 *Altri esercizi (1942–1971)*, Turin, Einaudi.
1974 *Esercizi di lettura*, Turin, Einaudi.
CORSINI, G.
1974 *L'istituzione letteraria*, Naples, Liguori.
CORTI, MARIA
1956 *P.J. De Jennaro: Rime e Lettere*, Bologna, Commissione per i Testi di Linguia.
1959 "Le fonti del *Fiore di virtù* e la teoria della 'nobiltà' nel Duecento," in *Giornale Storico della Letteratura Italiana*, CXXXVI, pp. 1–82.
1968 "Il codice bucolico e l'*Arcadia* di Jacobo Sannazaro," in *Strumenti critici*, 6, pp. 141–167; now in *Metodi e fantasmi*, pp. 283–304.
1969 *Metodi e fantasmi*, Milan, Feltrinelli.

1970 "Questioni di metodo nella critica italiana contemporanea," in *La critica forma caratteristica della civiltà moderna*, 1970 (see Anthologies, Collections).

1972 "I generi letterari in prospettiva semiologica," in *Strumenti critici*, 17, pp. 1–18.

1973 "Aspetti nuovi della prosa letteraria in prospettiva semiologica," in *Storia linguistica dell'Italia del Novecento*, "Atti del V Convegno Internazionale di Studi della SLI," Rome, Bulzoni.

1973a "Il genere *Disputatio* e la transcodificazione indolore di Bonvesin de la Riva," in *Strumenti critici*, 21–22, pp. 157–185.

1974 "*Strambotti a la bergamasca*, inediti del secolo XV: Per una storia della codificazione rusticale nel Nord," in *Tra latino e volgare: per Carlo Dionisotti*, Padua, Antenore.

1975 "Testi o macrotesto? I racconti di Marcovaldo di I. Calvino," in *Strumenti critici*, 27, pp. 39–60.

COSERIU, EUGENIO

1962 *Teoria del lenguaje y lingüistica general*, Madrid, Gredos (Ital. tr., *Teoria del linguaggio e linguistica generale*, Bari, Laterza, 1971).

DELBOUILLE, M.

1970 "À propos des origines de la lyrique romane: tradition 'populaire' et tradition 'clericale,'" in *Marche Romane*, 1, pp. 1–32.

DIJK, TEUN A. VAN. *See* Van Dijk, Teun A.

DOLEŽEL, LUBOMIR

1966 "Vers la stylistique structurale," in *Travaux Linguistiques de Prague*, I, Prague and Paris, Klincksieck.

DOUBROVSKY, SERGE

1967 *Pourquoi la nouvelle critique: Critique et objectivité*, Paris, Mercure de France, 1966 (Eng. tr., *The New Criticism in France*, Chicago, University of Chicago Press, 1973).

DRAGONETTI, R.

1969 "La littérature et la lettre (Introduction au *Sonnet en X* de Mallarmé)," in *Lingua e stile*, 2, pp. 205–222.

DUBOIS, JACQUES, EDELINE, F., KLINKENBERG, J.M., MINGUET, P., PIRE, F., TRINON, H.

1970 *Rhétorique générale*, Paris, Larousse.

1972 "Rhétorique poétique," in *Documents de travail* (Università di Urbino), s.B, 10, pp. 1–28.

DUCHET, C.

1971 "Pour une socio-critique, ou variations sur un incipit," in *Littérature*, 1, pp. 5–14.

DUVIGNAUD, JEAN
1967 *Sociologie de l'art*, Paris, Presses Universitaires de France.


ECO, UMBERTO
1962 *Opera aperta*, Milan, Bompiani.
1971 *Le forme del contenuto*, Milan, Bompiani.
1975 *Trattato di semiotica generale*, Milan, Bompiani.
1976 *A Theory of Semiotics*, Bloomington, Indiana University Press.
EDELINE, F. *See* Dubois, Jacques, et al.
ELIOT, T. S.
1951[3] *Selected Essays*, London, Faber and Faber.
1964[2] *The Use of Poetry and the Use of Criticism*, London, Faber and Faber.
ESCARPIT, ROBERT
1968 *Sociologie de la littérature*, Paris, Presses Universitaires de France.
ESCARPIT, ROBERT AND ROBINE, N.
1963 *Atlas de la lecture à Bordeaux*, Bordeaux, Centre de la sociologie des faits littéraires.


FABBRI, PAOLO
1973 "Le comunicazioni di massa in Italia: sguardo semiotico e malocchio della sociologia," in *VS* 5, May-August, pp. 57–109.
FILLIOZAT, PIERRE SYLVAIN
1972 "Une théorie indienne du langage poétique," in *Poétique*, 11, pp. 315–320.
FISCHER, L.
1973 "Rhetorik" e "Topik," in *Grundzüge der Literatur- und Sprachwissenschaft*, B.I., *Literaturwissenschaft*, Munich, Deutscher Taschenbuch Verlag GmbH u. Co KG.
FOUCAULT, MICHEL
1969 "Qu'est qu'un auteur?" in *Bulletin de la Société française de Philosophie*, July-September.


GADDA, CARLO EMILIO
1958 *I viaggi la morte*, Milan, Garzanti.
1974 *La meditazione milanese*, Turin, Einaudi.
GALLAS, H.
1971 *Marxistische Literaturtheorie*, Neuwied, Luchterhand Verlag GmbH.
GARAVELLI MORTARA, BICE
1974 *Aspetti e problemi della linguistica testuale*, Turin, Giappichelli.

GENETTE, GÉRARD
1966 *Figures*, Paris, Editions du Seuil.
1969 *Figures II*, Paris, Editions du Seuil.
1972 *Figures III*, Paris, Editions du Seuil.
GENINASCA, J.
1972 "Découpage conventionnel et signification," in *Essais de sémiotique poétique*, Paris, Larousse, pp. 45–62.
GENOT, G.
1970 "Analyse structurelle de *Pinocchio*," in *Quaderni* "Fondazione Nazionale Collodi," Florence.
GOLDMANN, LUCIEN
1964 *Pour une sociologie du roman*, Paris, Gallimard.
GOLINO, E.
1973 "Il mutamento nella storia e nella critica della letteratura: materiali per una sociocritica," in *Nuovi Argomenti*, 33–34, pp. 157–184.
1974 "Ricerca sociologica e letteratura: ideologie espressive e classi sociali," in *Nuovi Argomenti*, 40–42, pp. 186–229.
GOMBRICH, ERNST H.
1963 "Psychoanalysis and the History of Art," in *Meditations on a Hobby Horse and Other Essays on the Theory of Art*, London, Phaidon Press.
GRAMIGNA, G.
1975 *Il testo del racconto*, Milan, Rizzoli.
GRANGER, G. G.
1968 *Essai d'une philosophie du style*, Paris, Colin.
GREIMAS, ALGIRDAS JULIEN
1966 *Sémantique structurale*, Paris, Larousse.
1970 *Du sens: Essais sémiotiques*, Paris, Editions du Seuil.
GUGLIELMI, G.
1967 *Letteratura come sistema e come funzione*, Turin, Einaudi.
1974 *Ironia e negazione*, Turin, Einaudi.

HEMPFER, K. W.
1973 *Gattungstheorie*, Munich, Fink.
HOBSBAWM, ERIC J.
1974 "La funzione sociale del passato," *Comunità*, 171, pp. 13–43.

IHWE, J.
1970 "Kompetenz und Performanz in der Literaturtheorie," in

*Text, Bedeutung, Ästhetik*, Munich, Bayerischer Schulbuch Verlag.

1973 "Sprache—Struktur—Text—Literaturwissenschaft," in *Grundzüge der Literatur- und Sprachwissenschaft*, B. I, *Literaturwissenschaft*, Taschenbuch Verlag GmbH u. Co. KG (second edition used here, 1974).

JAKOBSON, ROMAN
1963 *Essais de linguistique générale*, Paris, Editions de Minuit.
1973 *Questions de poétique*, Paris, Editions du Seuil.
JAMESON, FREDRIC
1971 *Marxism and Form*, Princeton, Princeton University Press.
JAUSS, H. R.
1967 *Literaturgeschichte als Provocation der Literaturwissenschaft*, Constance, Universität Druckerei GmbH.
1970 "Littérature médiévale et théorie des genres," in *Poétique*, 1, pp. 79–101.

KLINKENBERG, J. M. *See* Dubois, Jacques, et al.
KOEHLER, E.
1967 "Les possibilités de l'interpretation sociologique illustrées par l'analyse de textes littéraires français de différentes époques," in *Littérature et Société* (*see* Anthologies, Collections).
KRAUSS, W.
1968 *Essays zur französischen Literatur*, Berlin and Weimar, Aufbau Verlag.
KRIS, ERNST
1962 *Psychoanalytic Explorations in Art*, New York, International Universities Press.
KRISTEVA, JULIA
1970 *Le texte du roman*, The Hague-Paris, Mouton.

LACAN, JACQUES
1966 *Ecrits*, Paris, Editions du Seuil.
LAUSBERG, H.
1949 *Elemente der literarischen Rhetorik*, Munich, Hueber.
1960 *Handbuch der literarischen Rhetorik*, Munich, Hueber.
LEFEBVRE, HENRI
1966 *Le langage et la société*, Paris, Gallimard.

LEVIN, SAMUEL R.
1962 *Linguistic Structures in Poetry*, The Hague-Paris, Mouton.
LOTMAN, J. M.
1970 *Struktura Khudozhestvennogo Teksta*, Moscow, Iskusstvo (Ital. tr., *La struttura del testo poetico*, Milan, Mursia, 1972).
LUPERINI, R.
1971 *Marxismo e letteratura*, Bari, De Donato.
LUZI, MARIO
1974 *Vicissitudine e forma: Da Lucrezio a Montale: Il mistero della creazione poetica*, Milan, Rizzoli.

MANDELSTAM, OSIP
1915–1930 *La Quarta Prosa*, Bari, De Donato, 1967 (a collection of his essays that does not correspond to a single Russian volume).
MAURON, CHARLES
1963 *Des metaphores obsédantes au mythe personnel: Introduction à la psychocritique*, Paris, Corti.
MINGUET, P. *See* Dubois, Jacques, et al.
MOUNIN, GEORGES
1969 *"La communication poétique" précédé de "Avez-vous lu Char?,"* Paris, Gallimard.
MUKAŘOVSKÝ, JAN
1966 *Studie z estetiky*, Prague, Odeon (Ital. tr., *Il significato dell'estetica*, Turin, Einaudi, 1973).

ONIMUS, JEAN
1973 Ruptures et interférences dans le langage poétique," in *Degrés*, 2, pp. 3–39.
ORLANDO, F.
1973 *Per una teoria freudiana della letteratura*, Turin, Einaudi.

PAGNINI, MARCELLO
1967 *Struttura letteraria e metodo critico*, Messina-Florence, D'Anna.
1970 *Critica della funzionalità*, Turin, Einaudi.
1974 "Il sonetto (A Zacinto): Saggio teorico e critico sulla polivalenza funzionale dell'opera poetica," in *Strumenti critici*, 23, pp. 41–64.
PETROCCHI, G.
1969 *Itinerari danteschi*, Bari, Adriatica.

PIRE, F. *See* Dubois, Jacques, et al.

POE, EDGAR ALLAN

1846 "The Philosophy of Composition," in *Graham's Magazine*, XXVIII (page references to *The Viking Portable Library: Edgar Allan Poe*, New York, Viking Press, 1945).

POZZI, GIOVANNI

1974 *La rosa in mano al professore*, Fribourg, Universitätsverlag-Editions Universitaires.

PRIETO, LUIS

1966 *Messages et signaux*, Paris, Presses Universitaires de France.

PROUST, MARCEL

(1954) "Le temps retrouvé," in *A la recherche du temps perdu*, III, B. de la Pléiade, Paris, Gallimard.


RIFFATERRE, MICHAEL

1960 "Stylistic Context," in *Word*, 16, pp. 211–244.

1971 *Essais de stylistique structurale*, Paris, Flammarion.

1972 "Système d'un genre descriptif," in *Poétique*, 9, pp. 15–30.

RISSET, JACQUELINE

1972 *L'invenzione e il modello*, Rome, Bulzoni.

ROBINE, N. *See* Escarpit, Robert.

ROSSI- LANDI, FERRUCCIO

1972 *Semiotica e ideologia*, Milan, Bompiani.

ROUSSET, JEAN

1973 *Narcisse romancier: Essai sur la première personne dans le roman*, Paris, Corti.


SARTRE, JEAN-PAUL

1947–1949 *Situations I, II, III*, Paris, Gallimard.

SCHÜCKING, LEVIN L.

1923 *Die Soziologie der literarischen Geschmacks-Bildung:* 1st ed., Munich, Gebr. Paetel; 2nd ed., Leipzig, B.G. Teubner, 1931; 3rd ed., Berne, A. Francke, 1961 (Eng. tr. of 3rd German ed., *The Sociology of Literary Taste*, Chicago, University of Chicago Press, 1966).

SEGRE, CESARE

1969 *I segni e la critica*, Turin, Einaudi.

1974 *Le strutture e il tempo*, Turin, Einaudi.

SERPIERI, A.

1973 *T.S. Eliot: le strutture profonde*, Bologna, il Mulino.

1975 *I sonetti dell'immortalità*, Milan, Bompiani.

SHKLOVSKY (SKLOVSKIJ), VICTOR B.
1925 *O teorii prozy*, Moscow, Federatsiia (Ital. tr. of the 1929 edition, *Una teoria della prosa*, Bari, De Donato, 1966).
STAROBINSKI, JEAN
1965 Rispòsta a "Inchiesta su 'Strutturalismo e critica,'" edited by C. Segre, in *Catalogo 1965*, Milan, Il Saggiatore.
1970 "La relation critique," in *L'oeil vivant II*, Paris, Gallimard.
STEMPEL, W. D.
1971 "Pour une description des genres littéraires," in *Actele celui de-al XII-lea congres international de linguistică si filologie romanică, Bucarest 1968*, 2 vols., Bucharest, II, pp. 565–570.
STENDHAL
1832 "Projet d'article sur *Le Rouge et le Noir*," in *Romans et Nouvelles*, I, La Pléiade, Paris, Gallimard, 1956.


TAVANI, G.
1972 "Per una lettura 'ritmemica' dei testi di poesia," in *Teoria e critica*, 1, pp. 19–70.
TERRACINI, A. B.
1966 *Analisi stilistica: Teoria, storia, problemi*, Milan, Feltrinelli.
TODOROV, TZVETAN
1967 *Littérature et signification*, Paris, Larousse.
1970 *Introduction à la littérature fantastique*, Paris, Editions du Seuil (Eng. tr., *The Fantastic*, Cleveland, Case Western Reserve University Press, 1973; paperback ed., Cornell University Press, 1975).
1971 *Poétique de la prose*, Paris, Editions du Seuil.
1971a "Roman Jakobson poéticien," in *Poétique*, 7, pp. 275–286.
TRABANT, J.
1970 *Zur Semiologie des Literarischen Kunstwerks*, Munich, Fink.
TRINON, H. *See* Dubois, Jacques, et al.
VALÉRY, PAUL
(1957) *Oeuvres I, II*, Paris, Gallimard.
VAN DIJK, TEUN A.
1972 *Some Aspects of Text Grammars: A Study in Theoretical Linguistics and Poetics*, The Hague-Paris, Mouton.
WEINRICH, H.
1967 "Für eine Literaturgeschichte des Lesers," in *Mercur*, XXI, pp. 1026–1038.
WIENOLD, G.
1972 *Semiotik der Literatur*, Frankfurt a. M., Athenäum.

ZAMBARDI, A.

1973 *Per una sociologia della letteratura*, Rome, Bulzoni.

ZAMJATIN, E.

1920 *Tecnica della prosa* (texts unpublished in Russia), Bari, De Donato, 1970.

ZANZOTTO, ANDREA

1973 "Alcune osservasioni di Andrea Zanzotto a proposito del suo componimento *Gli sguardi i fatti e senhal*," in *Poetiche*, Catalogo del Festival Internazionale di Poesia, Ivrea, Edizione de *Poetiche*, no pagination.

ZUMTHOR, PAUL

1972 *Essai de poétique médiévale*, Paris, Editions du Seuil.

1972a "Jonglerie et language," in *Poétique*, 11, pp. 321–336.

1975 *Langue, Texte, Enigme*, Paris, Editions du Seuil.

# Index of Names

Names of authors and historical persons are in roman; those of literary and mythological characters are in small capitals. Pages in the Notes section are italicized.